PEDESTRIAN PAPERS

WALTER S. HINCHMAN

PEDESTRIAN
PAPERS

Essay Index Reprint Series

BOOKS FOR LIBRARIES PRESS
FREEPORT, NEW YORK

First Published 1928
Reprinted 1968

LIBRARY OF CONGRESS CATALOG CARD NUMBER:
68-54350

PRINTED IN THE UNITED STATES OF AMERICA

THESE papers appeared originally in 'The Forum,' over the pen-name of 'The Pedestrian,' and I feel somewhat of a plagiarist in claiming them as mine. About all I can say is that, except for a good many of the ideas and a multitude of quotations, they are not any one else's. Nevertheless, the Pedestrian soon grew out of hand, like an unruly child, and, what with his 'damnable faces' and plain-spoken notions, he said and did things for which I should take no responsibility, did my Stratford lawyer not advise me that

'in these cases
We still have judgment here.'

It is therefore as a curious mixture of author and incompetent guardian that I subscribe to his work.

W. S. H.

CONTENTS

CONTENTS

PEDESTRIAN PAPERS

PEDESTRIAN PAPERS

THE PEDESTRIAN MIND

PEOPLE generally walk because they cannot afford to ride. For my part, I have long cherished the notion that few of us can really afford to ride; and like most cherished notions, it has grown into a conviction with me. Of course a great deal may be said for walking, in a purely physical sense; it is not a mere accident of some passing civilization, like chariots and sedan-chairs, but is one of the few things, like loving and eating, which have been common to all generations of men.

But I am thinking rather of the advantages of *mental* pedestrianism. It is with some alarm, I confess, that I observe the increase in vehicular traffic of this mental sort. The pedestrian mind doesn't get very far in one day, to be sure, but it has ample opportunity to see where it is going. It proceeds slowly enough to observe and record. It can stop altogether when it gets tired — a great virtue truly, for it is not likely to mistake motion and sound for progress.

Then, too, your mind afoot is not confined to

3

the highroad; it may follow by-paths; it may even explore unbroken wilds; it is not bound to the automotive 'wheel of things.' I don't make much of the fact that it can climb a tree, for Fords, they say, can do that too, though I do say for it that it still looks like a mind after its arboreal excursion.

But the great advantage of the pedestrian mind, to my thinking, is that, while it makes retirement possible, it is not 'retired leisure.' It has to work to get on; it moves often with the great procession of mankind. It knows, on the one hand, the starry solitude, the high mountain where one may pray, and, on the other, the crowded highroad where the race is to be run 'not without dust and heat.'

Are you a both — ander?

'Which side are you going to take, Liberal or Conservative?' said a friend to me not long ago, as we approached a house of controversy.

'Why should I take either side?' I answered — 'especially when I am not sure what either means.'

'That's No Man's Land,' he said; 'you'll get shot if you don't take sides.'

Like most of us, my friend was an *either — or* person, brought up on the foolish proverb that you can't have your cake and eat it too. Why not a *both — and* state of mind for a change? It might be diverting to be both liberal and conservative; and in point of intelligibility, it would be emphatically lucid compared to the *either — or* position of most people who call themselves one or the other. For the great alternatives, opposites though they may once have been, seem to be fairly interchangeable nowadays. Liberty, for instance, would seem to get on about as well when it assumes the engaging rôle of Tyranny as it did when it paraded with Equality and Fraternity or when it 'inhered,' among our forefathers, 'in some sensible object.' What a slogan, Liberty and Tyranny, one and inseparable! Perish the thought! Very well, let the thought perish, but, Mr. Voter, meet the fact.

All a man has to do, it would seem, is to pronounce his notions good and loud, and we follow like sheep or attack like wolves. A senator comes out with the astonishing discovery that the next political issue will be between progressives and reactionaries. Some papers, it is refreshing to note, are serious enough to treat this *pronunciamiento* with the persiflage it deserves, but a great many editors, and their readers with them, are foolish enough to imagine that he has said something and so get themselves into a hopelessly *either — or* state of passion over it. Incidentally, even his hostile critics give him the sort of free advertising that Barnum loved. Men and women evidently must be forever taking sides and biting their thumbs across the street at one another, some-

5

times when there is no issue at all, at other times when the issue is 'highly unimportant to Gods and men.'

For instance, this altercation about Fundamentalism. I should have supposed that anything *fundamental* in religion had primarily to do with truth and its rock-bottom basis, but very likely that's just an odd fancy of mine; at all events, the disputants, unquestionably audible, have revealed that the fundamental thing is to decide whether your wife is descended from a monkey or from one of Adam's ribs. Most of the American people find it easy to take sides on this question. I don't. I'll admit it's disquieting to reflect that your wife's ancestry may be Simian — it's rather disillusioning when you thought you had married a goddess; awkward, too, to break it to the children; but I confess to as much discomfiture when I reflect that I may be wedded to a spare rib. Also there's an unpleasant suggestion of the charnel house; to this favor we knew we should come at the last, but to think of happy living men everywhere wedded to bones — pah! 'mine ache to think on't!' But that's a digression. The point is that the disputants are *either — or* people. How they bite their thumbs!

Now of course there's no objection to taking sides when you know what you mean and the cause is worth fighting for. Professor Root's

6

article on 'The Virtue of Intolerance' a few years ago was a fine rebuke to those vacillating creatures who fancied that because their brains were shallow they must be broad. They are still at large among us, but they are not *both — and* people just because they fail to be *either — or* people. In fact, they are really *either — ors* thinly disguised: they are so committed to the process of selecting alternatives that, after persuading themselves that they are not *either — or* bigots, they leap to the conclusion that they must be *both — and* prophets. Better to be frankly *either — or* than that, even if it does commit you to Simian frolic or to the conjugal felicity of a sarcophagus.

But in many matters, when you stop to think about it, a *both — and* attitude is salutary. For instance, why not believe in Capital *and* Labor? Why not believe in Science *and* the Classics? Why not revive the spirit as well as the letter of that fine old phrase, Business *and* Pleasure? Why not, even, believe in the Bible *and* Evolution? It's quite possible, too, that a *both — and* attitude, even in the closed shop of marriage, might enable us to endure the worse as well as the better, the sickness as well as the health. There's a good deal to be said for walking down the middle of the street. Flying vehicles look dangerous, but they really have a tender regard for pedestrians; they are not half so dangerous as the snares of the side-

7

walk. Clear calls may come, when one or the other side is the only place; but, till then, let us not rush to the wall merely for the sake of being on a side-walk.

Perhaps we may take counsel from the perennial boy, who replies, when asked whether he will have pie or ice cream, 'I'll take both, please.' That boy sees life steadily and sees it whole.

YOUTH AND AGE

YOUTH is in the saddle. Allan Hunter writes to that effect in the December 'Forum.' Clark Trow, risking at thirty the imputation of senility, girds at him in the January 'Rostrum,' to be sure; but it is not insignificant that 'The Forum,' arch-apostle of debate, does not appear to consider this a debatable question. Youth gets the main article — let the old dogs growl in the 'Rostrum' if they must! The case is closed; Youth is in the saddle.

That's what the other magazines seem to think, too, and the reading public, and even respectable middle-aged people, who foot the bills. How grotesque would appear to-day Bacon's suggestion in the 'New Atlantis' that those who deserve the greatest authority in the government should be old in years, and that the chief power should be in the hands of men who can boast thirty descendants. Instead, one seems to hear a cry that the chief power should be in the hands of young people, who can boast no descendant. And it never dismays us that haply not only Bacon, but all antiquity, from Abraham to Gladstone, might smile at *us*. No — the case is closed; Youth is in the saddle.

Even those egregious philosophers who refuse to consider the case closed are curiously committed to alternatives. They maintain that there is something to be said for Age *as against* Youth. It is the same sort of *either — or* imbecility that keeps our sex altercations going — Woman *versus* Man. There will come a time, no doubt, at this rate, when we shall be seriously considering whether the left, the 'pure idea' of *leftness*, is superior to the glorious concept of right; and in that bright day we shall probably be able to decide the vastly debated question, whether Cæsar was a greater man than Napoleon. Yet we smile, forsooth, over the mediæval worthies who were concerned to settle whether the Cherubim or the Seraphim were higher in the celestial hierarchy. No — the case is obviously closed; Youth must be in the saddle!

Even in better days (that is, better from the point of view of the egregious philosophers) Youth and Age have been usually treated as alternatives. The only difference is that hitherto Age has been in the saddle. Few subjects, moreover, have had greater attention, especially from the old men; and writers, taking their cue from Cicero, have till recently decided that there may be consolations and dignities in old age which compensate for short breath and tottering knees. Raleigh, to be sure, and those Elizabethans who never grew up, wrote of old age and death with the profound dismay of youth in a graveyard. And when the pendulum swung the other way, solemn folk like Jeremy Taylor, who apparently forgot that they ever were children, derived a dismal exhilaration from warning the young that 'the clock strikes and reckons on our portion of eternity.' Charles Lamb, of course, remained a gentle rebel to the end; even when he settled in what he called 'this vale of deliberate senectitude,' he 'resented the impertinence of manhood.' Generally speaking, though, the old men have for centuries protested that Age has virtues no less renowned than Youth.

Then comes Browning and goes them one better. Age, he cries, is not only as desirable as Youth, but far better; indeed, Youth has no point without Age to crown it — 'the last of life for which the first was made.' Perhaps he protests a little too much, but he does give the old folk a battle-cry. Stevenson, in certain moments, liked no doubt to look forward and picture the placidity of himself by the fire — when he should 'remember the faces of women without desire and the deeds of men without envy.' But taking his cue from Browning, he preferred generally to sound the brave note of the high youthful heart even in the face of bodily dissolution. He has had perhaps as much influence as any one in setting up the popular ideal of 'young at sixty.' It is a pretty delusion, this, that if you will, you can be young at sixty. It is a romantic way of disposing of one of the alternatives. Presto! Age shall be transfigured into Youth. Whatever virtues it has are nothing, are mere consolation prizes, compared to the shining glory of Youth!

How much of a delusion this theory is may be seen if we reverse the picture. We swallow readily enough the idea that it is possible and altogether fitting to be young at sixty, but how about being old at sixteen? Yet why not? It's just as reasonable when you come to think of it. The first is a pretty picture — grandma stepping on the gas, and grandpa tempering his conversation to adolescent nonsense — but how would it look if Betty forsook her glad youth at sixteen for the knitting serenity of grandma, or if Roger settled into mature wisdom in his freshman year? We should not like it. We don't want it — and so we think it absurd. But we forgive grandma and grandpa their spectral attempts at rejuvenation. We even applaud them. It's all they can do, poor dears. They have abandoned the case for Age. They have left themselves only a pathetic imitation of Youth.

The trouble, I suspect, is not wholly that Youth is in the saddle, but is rather that Age has taken riotously to kiddie cars. For the old folk certainly over-act their part. Pretending to be about sixteen, they put on the charming *insouciance* of six. They forget all about the *teen* that marks your

genuine adolescent. No wonder serious young
men and women feel that they alone must run the
world. Yet the amazing thing is that when the
old people sit down solidly like old people and talk
about grown-up things out of their deep experience and in their own language, instead of in the
patter they mistake for a symbol of Youth, the
young people (not so dreadfully stupid, after all)
are only too eager to gather round and listen.

But this sort of normal blessedness is not likely
to return, except in isolated cases, so long as we
persist in the notion that Youth and Age are
separate, antagonistic states of being — or in the
more fatuous delusion that Age can be transmuted
into Youth. If we could realize that they are, after
all, as we usually think of them, mere abstractions,
conveniences of the pinchbeck philosopher, we
might the sooner realize that in actual experience
they are not separate, but make up a continuous
performance in the life of each individual. The
virtues of one predict or reflect the virtues of the
other. There is no time when one ceases and the
other begins. It is a one-act show; the curtain
never drops till the end of the play.

May our old men have the courage, then, to be
sixty at sixty — to substitute wisdom, rather than
nonsense, for senility. When they do, it is a fair
venture that the young will again seek their advice. Only a *both — and* state of mind can make

anything of the complicated civilization we have contrived for ourselves. For the young men need the old men — *in their right minds*. As a rustic philosopher commented when I sounded him on this idea, 'Well, I guess it all comes down to this: if the old men had a little more say just now, the world wouldn't go raound quite so fast — and I misdoubt that's about what she needs.'

COME on, let's walk; it's only three miles.'

Thus I recently to a companion, who compromised by hiring an automobile and who punctuated the journey with hilarious queries regarding my sanity. I replied with an aloofness which my friend finally mistook for prayer; but in point of fact I was 'experiencing' a fable, which ran somewhat like this:

Two men once considered making a journey. 'Let us go speedily by rail,' said one.

'No,' said the other, 'let us walk. I for one shall have to walk, since I cannot afford to ride.'

Some time later they met at their common destination. 'Well,' said the man who rode, 'how have you fared?'

'Splendidly,' answered the man who walked. 'I have just now arrived.'

'Indeed?' said the man who rode. 'I on my part have attended to all my business and have had time as well to examine the many wonders of this great city. You must surely count yourself unfortunate that you had to walk.'

'Not at all,' replied the man who walked. 'While you have an empty pocketbook and a cinder in your eye, I have a full heart and a flower in my buttonhole.'

'Yet if you could have afforded it, you would have ridden, wouldn't you?' asked the man who rode.

'That's the worst of it!' said the man who walked.

Out upon such cynicism! Is there nothing, then, but poverty to be argued in favor of walking? Apparently not even that, with most people, if we may judge from the numbers whom poverty liberates from the thralldom of riding and who nevertheless earnestly supplicate a lift.

Be that as it may, there would seem to be two schools in regard to locomotion. The one says, 'Never admit the possibility of walking, even hypothetically.' The other takes for its motto, 'Walking is perfect freedom.' The first school has a considerable waiting-list; the second is perpetually on the point of closing its doors for lack of patronage. I confess (or boast, if you like) that I am an alumnus of the less popular institution. At alumni gatherings we are somewhat forced to console ourselves with memories of an illustrious past, with reassuring glances from the portraits of such 'old boys' as Hazlitt and Stevenson (De Quincey, I believe, was only a 'special' and never quite in good standing), but a few of us are pledged, if the threat of closure continues, to return and take the course all over again — just to keep the old school going.

Francis Bacon and Mr. Wylie, practical men, extol walking for the health, but that seems to your true pedestrian a feeble justification of God's second greatest gift to man — a gift so great that without it (I speak now with the prejudice of my school) the greater gift may 'fust in us unused.' Still, ignoring the antiquated argument that God's gift is probably superior to man's inventions, ignoring too the fact that, though one can always walk where one can ride, one cannot do the reverse; passing over the antiquated and the incontrovertible, I can nevertheless find only speed in favor of any form of locomotion on land other than walking. When you walk, you have no machine to repair, no horse to stable; and if you break down, you have nothing but yourself to lay by for reconstruction. Bless you, you may break down at any moment, sitting inglorious in your automobile; well, then, you might as well break down without encumbrances and enjoy some philosophic moments by the roadside while you wait for a lift: there is nothing like an accident in solitude to quicken a man's philosophy. Think, on the other hand, of the vexation of your machine's breaking down (or your horse or your bicycle) while you rage hard by in impotent good health. It is bad

17

enough to sit crippled by the way while you con-
template a perfectly good bicycle at your side, but
to my mind it is much worse to accompany a dis-
abled bicycle along a sandy road.

For walking 'gregarious in a troupe' there is little to be said — except it be on military business.
Some one is sure to walk too fast or too slow or to
talk too much or too little or to make a party of
it. If progressive cogitation is thus forbidden, the
joy-ride has its advantages. Similarly, there is not
a great deal to be said for walking to and fro,
though that has its benefits if you are alone or
with one congenial companion. The rhythm of
your feet sets your minds and tongues in order:
conversation may progress instead of flutter. But
if you are alone, as Stevenson has so well pointed
out, and especially if your feet take you over the
hills and far away, you enter mysteriously into the
great fellowship of the Open Road. Alone, you have
plenty of time for meditation, and, hungry at the
end of the day's journey for companionship, you
are in a receptive mood for those brief but priceless
meetings which only trampers know.

I remember a Surrey gardener whom I met in a
little inn near Wastwater, a fellow with a benediction in his eye; we drank a glass of sacramental
milk at the parting of the ways — but that is another chapter.

Even your mountain-climber, if he returns always to the same inn at night, however perilous his rock-scrambles, never gets the same profit of the road as your tramp pedestrian. He cannot escape the atmosphere of homecoming, of expected things, of routine; every one else at the inn may have done exactly the same things as he; he is but a kind of glorified villager. The others have plucked the heart out of his mystery. But the true traveler is a kind of miniature Ulysses: he must press on — 'leave here the fatted cattle!'

This sense of superiority, of wide experience and advancing purpose, which your true pedestrian feels, is happily offset by a humility unknown to your homing walker. The latter may easily outstrip the young men of his small community; it is no feat to be first in Capel Curig or Franconia Notch. And if he feels indisposed, there is no eager, forward-seeking heart to prevent unworthy sloth. Your gentleman tramper, on the contrary, has seen cities and men — himself often least! — and is washed clean of small, provincial pride. Moreover, he cannot pick his day; he must take 'the rainbow or the thunder.' Nor can he adequately experience the humility on any feet but his own. It is not enough to be a traveler; he must be a tired traveler, with a respect for distance.

'And what should Master Gauger play
But *Over the hills and far away?*

19

'Whene'er I buckle on my pack
And foot it gaily in the track,
. . . . .
'Oh, I do think, and so do you,
It is the tune to travel to.'

That is our school song, written by Master Robert Louis Stevenson just before his graduation. It is the true litany of locomotion, sung not with clacking, cacophonous valves, but with the high heart of youth. And as we go forth from our little school, our kind teacher stands at the door with his words of cheer.

Go forth, he seems to say; go forth — preferably alone — and you shall find it; by quiet pools under the early dawn, by turbulent cataracts, on steep mountain ledges, in deep noon-day woods, on the open road. Not on the first day, perhaps, nor yet on the second or third, but after many days, when your precious body has grown indifferent to the stings and bruises of an all-day's tramp, when your cramped soul has been invisibly searched out and set in order — then you shall find it; and it is called Peace, the Peace of God, which passeth understanding, which passeth any poor explanation of mine.

THE PERMANENT ROOSEVELT

A GOOD many people are expressing their opinion of Lord Charnwood's 'Roosevelt' nowadays, yet, to my quadrupedantic way of thinking, most of them are wrong. Blind lovers of Roosevelt usually welcome another word in praise of their hero and let it go at that; blind haters of him put their busy fingers on little discrepancies here and there; and the irreproachably judicious get out their scales again. Now to my mind the conspicuous but only merit of the book lies in Lord Charnwood's ability to see the political figure of Roosevelt from a distance and thus to recognize, in a consistent picture, that his hero's mistakes were, after all, the defects of his virtues.

But this is not the permanent Roosevelt. Lord Charnwood pictures a great political figure, but without those human distinctions which in his lifetime made him a contagious personality and which among future generations will give point to his particular kind of greatness. Jefferson was no doubt a greater statesman, Lincoln a greater president; Cleveland was probably a greater executive; but no American since Franklin has been so great a man. Captain Burke, formerly one of

Roosevelt's New York police, said to the President's sister: 'Do you remember the fun of him, Mrs. Robinson? It was not only that he was a great man, but, oh, there was such fun in being led by him.' *Not only* that he was a great man! I wonder if Captain Burke knew that his leader was a great man partly, perhaps largely, because of 'the fun of him.'

'Manners maketh man.' Lives of great men may remind us that we can make our lives sublime, but primarily they remind us that the chief requisite of greatness is to be human. Already the political sagacity and courage of Lincoln are fading into the background, while the human personality emerges more and more to fill our minds and hearts and to fire our imaginations. Roosevelt the political figure is of the moment; the next generation will want, rather, evidences of what Roosevelt's sister-biographer calls 'his loyalty and tenderness of heart,' of what Captain Burke calls 'the fun of him.' Biographers usually make a stuffed Indian of their subjects — in spite of the evidence, in the Gospels, in Benvenuto Cellini, in Boswell, in Trevelyan, that the human story is the only permanent thing. We take our hats off to a political figure, but we *follow* a man. You can't quite make a stuffed Indian out of Roosevelt yet — he is still living in too many hearts. Also, a colorless *effigies* is no doubt useful in its way, like those busts of Cæsar and Socrates that used to adorn the schoolroom brackets. But we need more portraits of the astonishing and lovable *person*. We who knew him need them; posterity, who can know him only through books, will be impoverished without them.

Some of these portraits already have been drawn. 'My Brother Theodore Roosevelt,' by Mrs. Robinson, and 'Theodore Roosevelt's Letters to His Children' give us the beginnings of the gallery that we need. 'The Many-Sided Roosevelt; An Anecdotal Biography' and John J. Leary's 'Talks with T. R.' belong also in the gallery; and there are several little pen-and-ink sketches that must go in. But the walls are still almost bare. One biographer even apologizes for considering humor one of Roosevelt's merits, and makes nothing whatever of his voracious zest for it. We can't hang that picture!

Roosevelt's humor was not an occasional guest, for moments of relaxation. It attended his whole life. 'The fun of him' was intimately bound up with his intellectual vigor, his restless activity, and his 'tenderness of heart.' Suppose he had confided political secrets to me (he certainly was not guarded in his utterances, for he talked with bewildering indiscretion; but suppose I had been a political somebody in his life) — I think that, even then, the important thing would have been, not the

23

political secrets, but the restless vigor, the astonishing variety of interest, and the almost carnivorous humor. I say 'almost carnivorous,' but there was as much soul as flesh in it (hearty would be the word if we had not worn it out). We may as well grant that his sagacity, honesty, and courage had something to do with his success, but it was the more personal, human qualities which made people love and follow him.

Among these qualities none was more striking than his readiness on all sorts of subjects. His amazing absorption of reading matter is common knowledge, but there is one story in connection with it which, I believe, has never had much circulation. The late Barrett Wendell used to tell how he one day met a colleague in great perturbation of mind. The President, it appeared, was going to write an article on 'Old Irish Literature' and had asked Wendell's colleague to do him the favor of looking it over in manuscript. Of course he could not refuse the President, but — well, Roosevelt was a many-sided man, to be sure; still, it was hardly likely he had more than a superficial knowledge of the subject; he was certain to make dreadful mistakes, if not of fact, at least of opinion, in compressing so difficult and unfamiliar a subject into a magazine article. Not long after, Professor Wendell met the same colleague, this time delighted. Roosevelt, it appeared, had made an ex-

24

cellent job of it, an astonishingly good job —
astonishing indeed when he must have done it, so
to speak, with his left hand while he was at the
same time doing an astonishingly good job at
running the nation with his right.

After a busy morning, he would — but perhaps
I had better say *how* busy. I don't know when it
began, but by nine o'clock he had ridden horse-
back or taken a long tramp, eaten breakfast, and
read through a veritable pile of magazines and
newspapers. The reading alone would have killed
the morning for an ordinary mortal. If a few
minutes still remained before Mr. Loeb arrived at
Sagamore Hill, the President joined his family on
the porch, rocked hard, and talked harder. Then
till lunch he was closeted with Mr. Loeb or with
visitors, but closeted with the door open, so that
one passing could see him, usually on his feet,
dictating as strenuously as he talked in public.
He seemed to have time for everybody. He might
be dictating an important letter to Mr. Root.
Just as likely he was dictating a letter of genuine
gratitude to an old soul in Kansas who had sent
him a trumpery gift with her compliments and the
announcement that she had seven children; or
perhaps he was answering, as if it really mattered,
the letter of a little English boy who had written
suggesting that the American President should
have a bodyguard like King Edward's. They did

25

really matter to Roosevelt, these letters; for he was always interested in human contacts.

After such a morning, he talked his way through lunch, sometimes perhaps to keep the conversation where he wanted it if there were political guests, but more often, I suspect, for the same reason that Burke talked — 'not from a desire of distinction, but because his mind was full.' People representing all sorts of interests — political, business, ecclesiastical, academic, diplomatic — sat at his table nearly every day; yet, oftener than not, he knew more about their subject than they. I wondered at first if so much talk was not skillful bluffing; he might do it for a while, but surely he could not keep it up. It was fabulous, preposterous. But he stood the test day after day — routed us all over and over again, always with delicious good humor, incidentally ran the nation with unusual vigor, and wrote articles on 'Old Irish Literature' with his left hand! And so far only half the day has been accounted for! He had only just begun to fight.

This vigor and versatility were astonishing; but what made the conversation engaging, really memorable, was not its range, but its humor. He delighted in picturesque phrases. Not a 'phrasemaker,' never 'precious' in his English, he had, rather, an Elizabethan exuberance of phrase. He rarely spoke of a person without adding a telling

26

description; that was part of the 'fun of him.' I remember his speaking of one of the Secret Service men as 'Craig, that excellent fellow with the prize-fighting past.' Plain 'Craig' wouldn't do, not merely because he was 'excellent' (as indeed he was), but because Roosevelt's imagination would not brook the mere colorless name. He nearly always had more than the bare name for his children — sometimes a hilarious epithet when he was particularly affectionate. Which reminds me. One very solemn Senator I remember: a man who did not understand the 'headlong humor' of Roosevelt's phrases. On the day in question the President was late for luncheon, and Archie, aged eight and conceded to have special powers over his father, was sent into the study to act as bait. Before long they came impetuously forth, the President chasing Archie and shouting with melodramatic venom, 'You abominable little rascal! You incorrigible scamp!' Consternation of the solemn Senator, who glanced nervously at Mrs. Roosevelt — as who should say, 'You are smiling, madam, as if you approved of this strange behavior.' The President took the situation in at once and insisted on an *encore*. Rushing again at Archie, he repeated his lines, 'You abominable little rascal! You incorrigible scamp!' Further consternation of the solemn Senator as Archie was caught by this carnivorous creature. But Archie was only hugged, not eaten, and seemed to understand perfectly.

Surely, among all the people who knew Roosevelt intimately there must be some one to write the 'Life' posterity will need. Why should such some one not give up his present probably trivial occupation and set about it? Walt Whitman is reported to have said to his biographer, 'Put in all the damns, Horace' — by which he meant, of course, the ugly as well as the pretty, the plain unvarnished facts. So we must have the whole Roosevelt — the 'recall of judges' as well as the call to a 'square deal,' the ruthless treatment of an old friend as well as the splendidly ruthless treatment of himself. So also we must have the complete political record.

But with these things, and still to be imperfectly pieced out from the few portraits in our gallery, must go the story of his scientific and literary achievements, and especially the amazing record of his human contacts — the picture that shows his vigor and versatility, 'the fun of him,' and his 'loyalty and tenderness of heart,' the picture of the astonishing and lovable *person*.

For this last is the great, the permanent Roosevelt.

THE NEW ERA

THE other day I met a New Woman. She told me she was. To be sure, she had all the outward and visible signs of her species, but as we conversed (*perversed* were a more accurate word), I began to wonder whether she was quite so new as she thought she was. She was emancipated, she told me several times, from what she called Victorianism. '*From* that, yes,' I replied, glancing nervously at her costume, 'but *to* what? Whither, pray?'

She told me: 'To public life' (I perversed about Julia Ward Howe). 'To a new philosophy of life, based on the discovery of sub-conscious complexes' (I found it in my heart to ask if she had read 'Silas Marner'). 'To a new interpretation of sex relations, which recognizes "suppressed desires"' (I muttered of Godwin and Goethe). 'To a new religion, based on communications with the spiritual world' (I gestured toward 'Mr. Sludge the Medium'). 'To Communism' (I made an inarticulate face).

She finally persuaded me, quite against her will, that the things she called new were nearly all the logical conclusions of dear old Victorian beginnings, or older. Furthermore, when a woman, like a motor car, tries to go in two directions at once, disintegration is likely to set in. New Women are usually old.

But the New Woman is only a pretext. I confess that a lingering Victorian chivalry makes me feel a bit of a cad to have taken her rather than a male 'vile body' for my vivisectional practices, but science may not play favorites, and she *is* a fair symbol of our so-called New Age. For it often strikes me, as I pursue my pedestrian course, that this New Era, everywhere flaunted in our faces, is in reality the breaking-up of the Old. When people begin to dress old ideas up in new clothes, decadence, not renaissance, is at hand. If we are surging forward in a new era, there must be positive signs. But what do we see?

On all sides the ruins of the nineteenth century. Wireless telegraphy may be a new fact, but it is not a departure in kind. Indeed, Marconi is the logical conclusion of Morse, just as the Leviathan is predicted by the Great Eastern. Similarly, George Eliot and Hawthorne and Hardy foreshadow the problem novel. Our drama is perhaps new, at least in English-speaking countries, but new in form, rather than in thought: Bernard Shaw and Galsworthy do not hold extreme views so much as views *in extremis*. And to be what gets called a 'romantic ironist' is merely to be a deflated Meredith. Or — surely the pretense of some of our very modern poets and novelists to discover new emotions, as if there were such, is a *fin de siècle* gesture — no *aube* in that!

Any modern Diogenes, with his ever-ready lantern, finds little difficulty in revealing the same progression (if not progress) in other fields. Wilberforce slopes by green degrees to Bryan. Advertising develops into propaganda; Barnum prepares the way for Mr. Bok. In religion the churches are fighting the old battles over again. Neo-Puritanism had begun its noisy career before there were Chautauquas to promote it or Sinclair Lewises to revile it; it may be lovely or hateful, but it is not new. Or turn to the political field and behold the last vestiges of party government. Does any one really suppose that the *blocs* represent a new political principle, not just the *disjecta membra* of party government? It won't do any good to pretend that disintegration is integration by calling it 'new.' Even Communism is turning pink; it already suspects that it is the culmination of the French Revolution, not the red dawn of a new era. And the spirit of Napoleon, 'on a little mound,' looked down upon the Congress at Versailles and rubbed his eyes and wondered whether it wasn't Vienna and 1815. 'No,' chuckled the shade of Bismarck, nudging his elbow, 'Berlin and 1878.'

After all, what could be more indicative of decay, not growth, than our disposition to analyze

31

and criticize? The astonishing thing, really, is that we look in the glass and mistake ourselves for something brand new, instead of recognizing ourselves for what we are — the funeral baked meats. In the rapturous youth of our era we believed not only that Evolution was

'Climbing after some ideal good,'

but we comforted ourselves with faith:

'Thou wouldst not leave us in the dust.'

Now, in our senility, we appear to have abandoned heaven — what more natural when we had abandoned hell? For a while we took heart from the illusion that we were supermen; then, as disillusion set in, we began to wonder whether, instead of our abandoning heaven, heaven hadn't perhaps abandoned us: we are heirs to a disquieting feeling that a wise Deity might not only leave us in the dust, but might profitably step on us. A New Age, forsooth! The ashes of the phœnix, but where is the new bird?

But are there *no* signs of a new era? Personally, I harbor a private suspicion that a New Age *has* been born. Nature has certainly been in gigantic travail — enough to bring forth two new ages. I haven't seen the youngster yet, only heard him — a vociferous, unruly child. I get the impression that his parents, in the present domestic situation, have been unable to secure a competent

32

nurse. But, as I haven't seen him and am only
slightly acquainted with his family, I can't say
just what he is like. I *can* say, though, that he
isn't Freud, or Spiritualism, or the Movies, or
Radio, or Socialism, or Vers Libre, or Feminism,
or any other last enchantments of the nineteenth
century. And let's not forget, if the Old Age *is*
dead, that we have a body to bury; we have not
yet disposed of the 'intolerable residue.' And
after that, I suspect, we shall still have a stubborn
ghost to lay.

By the way, I have a strong suspicion that it's
her, not *him*.

GARDENING

MOST people make an orgy of their vacations. Their idea of relief from work is to buzz along in a cloud compounded of dust and oil ('picture ahead') for two stricken weeks — or longer if pocketbook and constitution allow. Then, when the allotted time and they are exhausted, they substitute the clack of the typewriter for the clack of the valve — and buzz some more.

Now I trust I am not so fatuous as to suppose that any special merit lies in the singularity of my vacations; in fact, I wish I might convert some of my friends and enemies to my ways. For from April to November — and indeed more or less through the winter — I take a vacation every day, in my back yard. I wish that I might call it a garden. My wife and I do so call it to one another, but in our hearts we know all along that it is a back yard. We too have heard of the English gardener who, when asked how long it took to make such turf as he was mowing in the close of Magdalen College, replied, 'About three hundred years.' Alas, my wife and I have been at it for only fifteen years; 'let us be lowly wise.' Furthermore, there is a tidy character, a weedlessness, an absence of ash-cans and clothes-lines, about a proper garden. It is not insignificant, though it is perhaps sad, that the honest American has to confess to a back yard.

Still, though we may not have a real garden (the kind, say, that God or Francis Bacon had in mind), the process which goes on in our rear enclosure *is* gardening — gardening from April to November and chopping wood through the winter. And as we toil, we do take comfort from the assurance that 'God Almighty first planted a garden.' Perhaps it is not a blasphemous supposition that, when Eden was new, it also had weeds that needed pulling and cats that devastated seed beds and sour soil that gave the grubs a chance. We know that the father of all cutworms made his home there; and if Charles Dudley Warner was right when he asserted that witch grass was original sin, there was certainly 'some' crop of it in that first and famous garden. What is more, we note that though Adam was not allowed to dig in Eden, the chief lesson he learned in his education there was to dig. 'Here, Adam,' we may imagine the Angel as telling him, 'this Eden is a model, in spite of its weeds and cats and cutworms and witch grass; there without are waste places and caterpillars innumerable. Dig, that the waste places may become a garden; and wheresoever thou discernest a caterpillar — or, more particularly, a cutworm — "smite, smite, in the name of God!"'

Observe, please, that I write not of gardens, but of gardening. Gardening, like education and culture, is a process, not a finished product. Unfortunately this idea does not seem to have got into the heads of many people. Gardens there are aplenty, with garden clubs and garden parties and garden goats, and all the delightful harmless things that go with them. Lots of people like to have gardens; they condescend to pick flowers and to do a little weeding — even enjoy getting their hands and shoes dirty; and they grow so keen that they read the catalogues till they can flourish the scientific names and distinguish a dozen kinds of gladioli, or irises, or tulips, or roses. But what do they know of gardening? Ask the son of Adam who works for them — *he* knows! He knows what it is to toil till the 'hinge in his back' rusts fast; he has crocked wireworms by the thousand and squashed cutworms by the million (quietly, methodically, courageously, as part of the God's work he is engaged in); he reeks gloriously of a strange mixture of sweat and whale oil soap and tobacco and sheep manure.

And he knows, too, the enduring joys of his task. First, that it will never be done; there is an inexhaustible demand for *him*. And he understands what indeed is the chief of gardening joys

36

— to gather seed and plant it, and transplant the seedling, and nurse it through its babyhood and guard its adolescence, till he sees it, through his own creative energy, live gloriously in a flower. Out upon your potted annuals, bought at the nearest florist's! With a southward-facing window and a cold frame or two, you can raise and make live all the flowers and vegetables you deserve to have. If you must have more, if you have become *addicted*, as I have, sell your automobile and build a little green-house. But then you will not need to be told to toil. You will have become one of us; you, too, will reek gloriously and develop the rusty hinge and kill the devil's creatures with your naked hands.

For the subtlest of all gardening joys lies really in the state of mind that is induced by toil. You can flutter in a garden, but you can't flutter at gardening. As the hours pass (not a few frantic minutes, but slow, silent, blistering hours), you gradually find yourself alone with a creation larger than you are. Your good wife, realizing that her blessed curse is to spin while you delve, leaves you to your silent labor; your disordered mind begins to sense a mysterious rhythm in which thinking and feeling are mutually inclusive (not exclusive, as they often are back there in the narrow house); and when at length the shadows lengthen and the busy world is hushed, you have seen and known things which pen cannot picture. You are no longer a mere wrangling mental mechanism; you have for a while been at one with creative energy.

Yet mere toil will not invite the Divine Presence — let us not be fatuous about that, either. Toil is only the first condition; for the labor must bring forth beauty — beauty of form and color — and that is a much harder condition. It is easy to be a mere ditcher; it's a different matter to be an artist. But God, we suppose, walked in Eden before it was quite finished; planted it *himself*; did, if he was the sort of God he appears to have been, himself pull the weeds and drive out the worms; knew how to 'toil terribly.' Perhaps, then, though we cannot boast a sward three hundred years old, God will look kindly on our baby gestures, will walk in our back yard some blessed day, 'when the eve is cool.'

THE PROHIBITION OF PREACHING

MISTAKE me not, reader. I am not thinking of the prohibition of liquor. One rarely *thinks* about liquor; one *feels*. Also, it is a dead issue. There are too many people who imagine there's nothing either right or wrong but drinking makes it so.

It is the principle of prohibition, rather, that occupies my mind. Morality depends on inhibitions; legislation on prohibitions. But morality is now in the discard. A forward-looking world is turning more and more to legislation, the modern substitute. For years our forbears talked about inalienable rights (quaint notion) and made the path of the millennium-seeker difficult. But nowadays only a few hopelessly antiquated people like Fabian Franklin and Agnes Repplier talk of our rights. A large number, to be sure, talk of our wrongs, but a great percentage of this number seem to be friendly to the fundamental principle of legislative prohibitions. If we got nothing else out of the conflict with Germany, we appear to have learned the deep implications of 'verboten.' Nor have we merely apprehended a great truth; rather, we have embraced it with the fresh ardor of converts. For the antiquated and really selfish desire to be saved, we have substituted the consuming passion to be forbidden. We have even written it into our Constitution: it has become a *right*.

It occurs to me, therefore, that this passion ought to be taken at the flood. The excellent principle of prohibition ought to be applied to activities even more pernicious than the manufacture, sale, and transportation of liquor. Take automobiles, for instance; test them by the same arguments that served us in the glorious campaign against rum. Indisputably they already kill more than John Barleycorn ever threatened to destroy. The money spent on them in a single day, I have computed, would feed — but I do not mean to press the case against automobiles; I might be accused of a pedestrian prejudice.

My animus, rather, is directed against the manufacture and sale of intoxicating ideas. In this case the arguments are even more irrefutable than in the case against liquor. For synthetic liquor never existed till necessity forced its invention, but artificial and substitute ideas, which cost a lot and make people go blind, flourish without excuse. People will drink in poisonous ideas with so little discrimination that only the most rigorous sort of prohibition can save the State.

Pray, do not suppose I jest. It is now plain sense, since we have by constitutional amendment

abrogated the fantastic delusions of our forefathers (to protect the rights of minorities), it is
now sweet consistency to step forward to further
reforms.[1] If I jest, it is with bitter scorn that we
should glow with pride over the prohibition of
liquor (a minor virtue) while we leave intoxicating
notions (a major vice) still unrestrained. We
make, to be sure, a pathetic pretense of action —
in our timid censorship of the theater and the
movie-palace, and in our weak restraint of persons
who openly foment conspiracy against the United
States. Why not strike at the root of the matter?
Why not prohibit preaching?

It would be tedious to rehearse now all the
arguments in the case, but when leagues and legislators take the question up, we shall no doubt hear
in detail pleadings strangely familiar. At times
we may even have to rub our eyes to make sure
that the question before the tribunal is preaching,
not rum — so familiar will the arguments be.
We shall learn of families broken by intoxicating
notions that inflame the passions, we shall hear of
morals perverted, of dogmas subverted, of malice
domestic and foreign levy — all set in motion by
the insidious poison of false prophets. The sta-

[1] I make little of the possible comment of some future his-
torian, noting the paradoxical position of a people who claim,
in a constitution or bill of rights, the *right* to be *wronged*; but
I ought in all fairness to confess that I hear the distant thunder
of his chuckle.

tistician will come into his own again. We shall
meet the economic argument against preaching —
too obvious to need expansion. We shall hear also
the humanitarian argument: pious souls will maintain that, as the prohibition of liquor — I mean, of
preaching — will do unquestionable good, *any*
violence to the Constitution or to antiquated
theories of liberty is justifiable. We shall hear the
other side, too. Plausible arguments will be put
forward by the ecclesiastical 'interests': we shall
be told that many people, for years accustomed to
their weekly sip of intoxicating notions, have a
right to consideration; it will even be argued, as it
was with liquor, that some people simply cannot
get along without it; probably there will be a
suggestion that sermons be limited to four per
cent — I mean four minutes. But the American
people will know how to meet these insidious pleas
dictated by self-interest.

Naturally no one will be foolish enough to attempt to prohibit listening. The league which
will be formed to suppress preaching will have to
rest content with an attack on the *sale* of intoxicating notions. That will, of course, leave a good
many priests in the pulpit. Besides those few who

'Cristes gospel trewely wolde preche,'

there will be the Quakers, who take no pay for
their wares; but it appears that they, having no

42

dogmas to defend, rarely find it necessary to deal in inebriating fictions. Then there will be the large number whose preaching is no more intoxicating than soda-water. The economic argument will get them in time, but that lies outside the present discussion. In addition, there will be no doubt a good deal of sermon-bootlegging; there are some people who *will* preach even if they have to do it at great risk. An alert federal service, however, should find little difficulty in keeping them beyond the twelve-mile limit; and since most of them have at least the minor virtue of a lodg'd hate and certain loathing against rum, they may go far towards converting the liquor pirates from their evil ways.

From the foregoing it will be seen that the main arguments are identical with those against liquor: clear, irrefutable arguments, that could be made into a watertight syllogism. But it must not be supposed that the law will be easy to pass. We shall have to reckon with a large number of people who will still hold preachers in sentimental reverence. They understand these things better in Russia. Here it may take years to wean the public from its slavery to the pulpit, though the signs of the times are not without hope. Again, the funds which sustained the crusade against liquor were subscribed largely by devoted church-goers; we can hardly expect financial aid from them in an

43

effort to prohibit preaching. Still, these objections must not be supposed in any way to invalidate the *logic* of the case against preaching; and, as for their obstructing the progress of beneficent legislation, they are not so formidable as they appear — since we have already established the fundamental *principle of federal prohibitions.*

It is with some hesitation that I dismiss the subject thus. It is a cause which touches the heart as well as the head. I would fain strike an heroic note, suggest a slogan for the call to arms. I realize, of course, that in our enlightened age we must not give way to evil passions. So, instead of crying, as did the brutal, uncivilized pamphleteer of the eighteenth century, 'Let us crucify the thieves!' — I feel that we should content ourselves with the gentler slogan: 'Let us stop their mouths with dust — with legislative dust!'

THE LABOR PROBLEM

'I T isn't the coffee, Steve, dear,' says Henrietta in the play.

Henrietta was half right. It wasn't the coffee, or the recurring and recalcitrant furnace, or the dreary details of the daily round. It wasn't even Henrietta's recurring and recalcitrant face, provocative of gloom as that might be. But it wasn't a 'suppressed desire,' either, as Henrietta supposed it was. It was a state of mind into which Steve and the rest of us get often enough. We need refreshment, the preacher tells us; we 'need to go apart into a high mountain to pray.' The narrow house has made us short-sighted and astigmatic; only clear air and open spaces will enable us to see life steadily and whole.

Feeling thus, perhaps even *thinking* thus, I listened the other night to a heated argument at the club. Years of pedestrian habits have given me a facility at slipping unobtrusively into groups where I do not belong. Usually I listen and am disregarded, as a piece of inoffensive furniture. This time, however, I had the temerity to speak; — mission furniture I had become, I fear, and not inoffensive.

45

The group — a business man, an economist, and a college professor — were discussing the Labor problem. Their arguments were familiar enough. The business man, frankly partisan, held that the only cure was to open the gates wide to immigration. The professor, a veiled partisan of Labor, felt that the solution lay in keeping the bars up, and he pleaded that to argue against protection of Labor was in effect to argue against a protective tariff. The economist exploded that notion quickly enough. In fact, his chief office appeared to consist in exploding other people's notions; but the professor, explosive in his own way, kept supplying him with fresh ground for statistics and calculations. Under this withering fire the business man had retreated to the admission that the issue between Capital and Labor was eternal, in the nature of things, and that therefore compromise was the only solution. 'There must be concessions on both sides,' he said with a new, philosophic tone.

'A sort of armed truce!' cried the professor. 'And when the issue comes up in a new form, what then?'

'Another compromise,' replied the business man.

'And more *concessions!*' The professor shouted it as if he meant 'concussions.' 'My soul, why must stupid people go through the sickening game over and over again? Why can't the issue be decided right once and for all?'

'Because it is an inevitable issue,' said the economist quietly.

'Inevitable!' exploded the professor. 'Just because capitalistic governments have been unable to solve the problem, you capitalists argue that it is insoluble.' Then followed a *Putsch* for Socialism, which the economist effectively silenced with more statistical machine-gun fire.

It was at this point that I made my unhappy sally. The professor, hoist with his own petard, was busy consolidating his retreat, and the business man, mistaking repetition for argument, had just stated again the eternal nature of the conflict and therefore the necessity of compromise, but with this difference, that it was Labor's turn now to make concessions and that the bars to immigration should be let down a good deal — in fact 'a whole lot.'

It was unfortunate that I did not for the moment recall that the business man's Christian name was Stephen — 'Mr. Jorrocks,' I had always called him. So it was a bad beginning when I said sweetly, 'It isn't the coffee, Steve, dear.'

Perhaps that was why he found it difficult to see any sense in my subsequent remarks. But I suspect him of having been committed already to a point of view, though he was positively open-minded compared to the irascible professor. But even the economist treated me with an obliterating mixture of contempt and statistics.

So, after a futile attempt to introduce another point of view, I went out a defeated man. But as I was not quite ready for interment, I resolved to go once more outside the city, to get away from the narrow house to a high hill and look across the years.

Possibly we pedestrians do not live wholly enough in a fleeting present. The driver of an automobile has to be terribly alive to the emergencies of the moment. Sometimes, though, there is a virtue in looking backward as well as forward. Sometimes, too, pedestrians pause on hilltops where they enjoy an extensive prospect; not just glance at it, but look long and often.

Not only has the modern conception of the universe become an accepted condition of popular thinking, but modern views regarding church, government, work, and play get accepted without question by the run of mankind. A few eccentric people, a few theorists and misfit idlers, protest in behalf of some odd fancy, the specious merit of which usually lies not in itself, but in its *difference* from 'accepted standards.' Here and there is a quiet scholar who knows better; here and there a prophet — usually crying in the wilderness; but the sane people, the people who think they make the world go round, are prodigiously committed to their immediate civilization. It is no doubt natural for them to be so. The long-haired Merovingians in their forests, as the Romans in their forum, probably accepted their passing experience as blandly as our modern 'two-fisted' men succumb to theirs. Naturally they are distrustful of panaceas — 'there ain't no such animal.' And they find Socialism and other experimental cures worse than the disease, so they muster conviction with repetition and hold that the disease is 'in the nature of things.' But it does at times look a little like pouring water through a sieve because you can't get it to boil.

Among these commitments, Europe and America have accepted the notion that society is in horizontal stratifications, with Capital in the top story and Labor in the basement. And a further part of the notion is that the only thing worth doing is to run upstairs — or, better yet, to glide up in the elevator. For the capitalist this means building new stories; for Labor it means getting control of the elevator. But suppose the stratifications were *vertical*; men could still satisfy their apparently incurable and no doubt laudable desire to keep going up and yet not interfere with the family in the flat above. Nor is it a wholly fanciful notion to imagine just such vertical stratifications of society. In that great period of history which we used to call 'dark' and now call 'middle' and may some day call 'light,' a man might rise to any height without invading another man's domain. The meanest cotter might become Pope; an artisan might become a great artist; but they could not become, nor did they greatly expect to become, kings or capitalists. Those were other classes, not above them in a business sense, but beside them. Then no doubt, as at all times, men coveted their neighbor's goods, but the conflicts between Labor and Capital were temporary and accidental. A comparison of the mediæval guilds with the modern unions tells the whole story — the one desirous only of safeguarding its own rights in its own home, with a roof against the sky; the other struggling from the basement to dispossess the people in the flats above.

Yes, the professor was right, my hilltop tells me, when he cried out against patched-up truces, but he was wrong, miserably wrong, when he imagined that the trick could be turned by legislation or that a new kind of government was the panacea. It isn't a question of tariff, or of the cost of living, or of equitable wages, or of immigration, or of competition — 'it isn't the coffee, Steve, dear'; it's a state of mind.

A state of mind, a 'way of life,' is not begotten of legislation. Nor yet of propaganda, though some people would appear to think so. Even education cannot produce it with certainty. It implies more than a mere *decision* about Labor, it implies a philosophy of life; and that means a revaluation of all sorts of things — indeed, a new civilization. A new state of mind may require a new state of soul.

But the economist is busy with graphs and charts; and the business man says we have a 'concrete issue' to face; and the professor still wants to try legislation. So I suppose we shall still go on pouring water through sieves. I am reminded of the Scot whose wife requested him to bury her in Carracuddy.

'No, Mary,' he said, 'I'll bury ye in Edinburgh; it's cheaper.'

'Sandy,' she cried, 'ye'll bury me in Carracuddy, else I'll haunt ye.'

'Mary, gin I maun bury ye in Carracuddy, I'll bury ye in Carracuddy — but I'll try ye in Edinburgh first.'

PROPAGANDA

AFTER my unhappy sally last month, when I sought to transform a futile Labor discussion from a vicious circle into a beautiful parabola, I have been condemned to the society of the club bore. My good friends, the business man, the economist, and the professor, treat me a little distantly, as if I might again interfere with some radiant game of theirs, and they glance across the room with unfeigned delight when they see me cornered with Exacticus. No ordinary club bore he! Not the kind from whom you turn furtively away, not one of those famous for his unfinished stories. Exacticus pins you down — spikes you down, in fact — and then sits astride your chest and finishes the job.

But the other night he did not mistake me for an antagonist, as he usually does; for he was full of a discovery he had recently made. The Society for the Extension of Christian Truth, he told me with many a chuckle, was nothing but the whim of a fantastic old gentleman to save the gullible public from the evils of organized exploitation.

'You see,' Exacticus said, 'the man in the street hasn't a chance when organization gets hold of him. He may resent the suggestions of advertisers at first, but he gradually succumbs to their magic. And even when he still dreams that he is holding the citadel, his wife is letting the enemy in at the postern gate. Now, sir, during the war mankind learned that the same principle could be applied to public policies. Organize, sell the idea to the people — then legislate. Any sensible man realizes the far-reaching implications of propaganda, but is powerless to stop it. While he writes an article that is read by seventeen high-brows, the militant minorities are circularizing the nation. So, sir, our little old gentleman realized that the thing to do was to fight fire with fire, to organize and circularize.'

'But why,' I asked, 'did he not join other organizations already in the field? There are such, I believe — organized to preserve our liberties.'

'Stupid!' retorted Exacticus with his usual precision. 'Most of them have axes to grind too. They are out for counter-legislation; with the best intentions in the world, they are combating half-truth with half-truth. But our old friend has no axe to grind whatever — his sole aim is to teach, to help the plain people to resist imposition in whatever form it may appear. He's a missionary.'

'That's the reason he puts "Christian" in the title of his society?' I queried with a grin.

'Not at all!' replied Exacticus contemptuously. 'He used to call it the "Anti-imposition Society,"

53

but he couldn't get a following. Now, with the new name, he counts his subscribers by the thousands. And after all, the exposure of untruth and half-truth is about the most Christian thing a man could do nowadays.'

'I suppose he's making money out of it,' I remarked cynically.

'I don't believe so. Printing and postage and office-rent cost a lot. But really, he himself is more of a discovery than his society. I'll take you to see him some day.'

Determined to see the strange old gentleman without Exacticus to edit him or to expose my imbecility, I visited the office of the Society for the Extension of Christian Truth the next morning.

The name of Exacticus, whom I mentioned, proved talismanic, and I was shown immediately into the rear office.

There sat the President — a lean little man, rather shabbily attired, looking, in his shirt-sleeves, much like the incarnation of editor, compositor, proof-reader, and printer's devil seen in some country newspaper offices. When he looked up, though, his eye was full of an eager light that carried his weariness easily. He showed me to a chair and soon warmed to his subject.

'Exacticus gave you rather a false impression,' he said. '*He* would like me to rage about in the political arena, but I have avoided it generally.

54

It is very hard to get at the whole truth of any political matter. Adding half a truth to half a truth doesn't give you a whole truth, you know, and I make it my primary principle to send out only information that I and my able assistants have tested till we *know* it is true.' (He gestured toward the girl in the front office and toward an energetic, wizened old lady who, I already noticed, seemed to have the rare faculty of communicating adequately without speech.) 'That of course rather precludes the political field, doesn't it? Though I realize that I shall have to do something there too if the society is to justify its name. Since well-meaning but mistaken minorities have been using propaganda to accomplish legislation — worse yet, to persuade the people that the Constitution should become a code of statutes — I have taken one or two flings at hoary lies adorned as truth. I neglected to attack the Eighteenth Amendment, I confess, for liquor has always repelled me (we all have our little idiosyncrasies, you know), but I am going for this proposed amendment to prohibit the teaching of evolution. I've got my coat off now,' he added with a humorous gesture at his attire.

'But how,' I asked, 'do you "go" for such a proposed amendment?'

'Well,' he said, 'it's not so simple as attacking untruthful advertisements. There I simply write,

55

"The Kleen Razor Company has lowered its prices; it has also lowered the quality of the steel in its blades." Then I send the statement to all members of the Society. They know I have no razor or whatever to sell them, and sooner or later, if I have enough members, they may make it hot for the perfidious manufacturers.'

'But I should think the business concerns would make it hot for you,' I said.

'They do,' he replied with a grim smile. 'Some of them are after me all the time. If I make a false statement, they'll get me. It's quite exhilarating. They have even tried to thug me.'

'How could you meet that?' I asked. 'Expose the municipal police?'

'Oh, no,' he laughed; '*they're* hardened to exposure. Also, the best police force in the world can't prevent artful thuggery. No, I've been lucky so far — and rather skillful with my hands and feet, though I may not look it.'

I recalled him to evolution.

'Oh, yes,' he replied. 'As I said, that's not a "straight proposition," like attacking the fraudulent advertisers. The thing to expose, you see, is not fundamentalism or evolution, but the mistaken notion that either of them is religion. That involves all sorts of prejudices and preconceptions; and most of the simple souls who belong to our Society are quite incapable of keeping the issue clear, without passion. All I can do so far is to sow seeds of information, but the crop is beginning to come. To many fundamentalists, of course, I seem to be supporting their side, and to many of the quack evolutionists, the bitter-ender scientists, I seem to be supporting their side, too. Naturally I take pains to attack neither, and as a matter of fact I don't mean to attack either, but in the end to liberate people from a narrow thraldom and, in a practical aspect, to convince them that such things cannot be written into law. It's a slow process, like all education, and the law may be passed before I get a large enough public or before I get that public enlightened. But that isn't going to make me frantic. I've taken my coat off, but, by your leave, I'm going to keep my shirt on.'

This old gentleman somehow appealed to a pedestrian mind. 'If it is not too bold a question,' I said, 'may I ask how you qualified for this work? It's stupendous!'

'By general failure,' the old gentleman replied matter-of-factly. 'I have been an electrician, a barber, an amateur lightweight pugilist, a salesman, and a college professor — of sorts. I have failed dismally at everything I have taken up. And I rather expect to fail at this, too — but — but it will be more exhilarating to fail in this way than ——'

57

'"All men strive, and who succeeds?"' I put in with a platitudinous grin.

'A pretty piece of poetry,' returned the old gentleman, 'but in point of fact, about half strive and two per cent succeed. What success I may be having, I lay to the little old woman. I am author and compositor, but she is editor and printer's devil. When we rented our office, her first purchase was a quantity of blue pencils and wastebaskets. God bless her!... Perhaps,' he added with a reminiscent look, 'I owe something to my experience as a barber; people have a way of confessing to barbers. I learned that the majority of people don't think; they just imitate thinking; but they do really feel, and the less they can understand their feelings, the more they believe in them.'

'What you say interests me,' I put in, 'the more so because Exacticus and I were talking of it last night. In fact, I once wrote a little attack on our recent indulgence in propaganda to produce legislation.'

'Did you?' cried the little man eagerly. Then, with a disappointed look, 'Oh, but I suppose you had no audience to speak of.'

'Not much, I fear; but one man evidently read it, for he wrote an answer, saying that the Pedestrian had gone astray, that any one ought to know that propaganda created "states of mind," which eventually developed into "public opinion," which in turn led to "legislation."'

'A hoary notion,' he replied. 'Propaganda may get people into a *state*, but rarely into a *state of mind*, and such states of feeling may coalesce into public *passion*. But public *opinion* is a very rare bird. It is just on this account that propaganda is the chief weapon of organized minorities. It's merely a grandiose form of advertisement: you can sell almost anything if you say it attractively and intensively. The American people are like a jury faced by unscrupulous lawyers and without a judge to instruct them.

'Why, don't you see,' he cried with animation, 'that this is the very thing I am attacking? I don't really care much whether the American people succumb to the perfidy of the Kleen Razor Company; but that is symptomatic. What I am after is the growing tendency to believe anything that's told you. Look at the Child Labor discussion. A lot of people for the amendment, a lot against it — most of them excited — and now comes a sober commission with the report that the evidence so far is too antiquated and too inadequate to be of value. Yet the partisans, the propaganda producers, pretended that the evidence was all in and conclusive.'

'But even if the evidence showed conclusively that conditions were very bad, would you believe in a Federal Amendment to —— '

'Ah, that's a different question, a matter of political theory. But come see me another time about that. My coadjutor there has twice signaled me to get rid of you and settle down to work.'

THE HUMAN VOICE DIVINE

THERE is no question that my animus against the movies springs partly from prejudice. Their nervous speed does not appeal to the pedestrian type of mind. They don't even warn you off from the pictures a self-respecting pedestrian ought not to look at; so that, during my annual attendance (just to avoid the appearance of prejudice), I never manage to avert my gaze in time to escape seeing the close-ups, rolling their eyes. They ought to blow a horn, to warn pedestrians.

But these are minor offenses. I might become subdued to these, if only some one would speak. In a movie palace I feel like the little slum girl sent for the summer to a New England farm. Halfway through the first meal she broke the steadfast silence with a passionate cry: 'For God's sake, somebody *speak!*'

Speech is more fundamental, I suspect, than our movie-men realize. Long, long ago a caveman desired a wife or food or the extinction of an enemy — desired it so fervently that he burst into rude, passionate grunts, into a kind of language. Then, no doubt, he suited the action to the word. Perhaps he acted first and suited the word to the action. I am skeptical about that, though, even to the extent of taking issue with Hamlet's advice to the players. What the cave-man said *after* the action expressed another emotion, very different from the first sensation of desire. But the real point is, not that speech precedes action, or that perhaps they are simultaneous, but that neither can get on without the other. Put your hands in your pockets, relax all your muscles, and try to say as you imagine it should be said some strong speech, such as Hamlet's

'Oh, all you host of heaven!'

or Falstaff's

'No more o' that, Hal, an thou lovest me.'

Or try to act it without speech. Do it before a mirror and get a close-up of yourself (rolling your eyes).

Well, to get on with the story — many years after the caveman's passionate grunts, a sophisticated person, under the urge of artistic creation, wished to represent dramatic episodes in some way that would give the illusion of reality. After a while he discovered that his pantomime, never quite genuine, always wooden, mechanical, even though the actors were *human* machines, took on greater reality when the actors spoke. Drama, as we understood it up to the close of the nineteenth century, was born. The prime necessity was perfect speech, provocative of action; speech which should embody the very soul of the emotion felt, which should impel a perfectly corresponding action, together transmitting, as mere speaking or mere acting, separately, could never do, the illusion of reality. Good acting was a necessity too, but the tone of voice was what really mattered, what impelled the acting.

Then comes scientific man with his new toy, the pantomime machine. That the majority of people are satisfied with the dumb-show acting of the machine is perhaps not remarkable. Already accustomed to prefer photographs to drawing and painting, undeniably susceptible to thrills and howlers, why shouldn't they prefer the feats of 'Doug' and the antics of 'Charlie' to the legitimate drama? We are most of us groundlings at heart, and Shakespeare would have had a hard run of it, even with an audience habituated to poetry, if he had had to compete with the marvels of the movie-stage. It makes me rather tired to hear the objection that the movies are cheap art. We get what we want; and if it comes to that, they compare well enough with the swaggering pre-Shakespearean tragedy, 'in King Cambyses' vein,' or with the cheap humor of Gammer Gurton, her needle lost forsooth till Hodge finds it in his trousers by sitting on it (close-up of Hodge sitting down — *and* rolling his eyes). In this respect, at least, they can improve just as easily as spoken drama can improve — when we want it.

Then there are the high-brow gentlemen who, like myself, insist that the soul of good drama lies in speech. Doug and Mary may burst into the 'sheer splendor of speech' as they jump from a Hollywood precipice, but all we get is the silent action and the gasp or guffaw, 'stepped down,' of the fat lady and the thin man behind us. Still, this objection may be in part overcome. In this age it is not difficult to imagine machines that will reproduce the whole thing, spoken as well as acted, with a precision that will leave little to be desired. Mr. DeForest has one now, he says; invented, so to speak, while we talk.

I don't even worry over the waste of time and money on the movies, dreadful as they are; for they are not so bad as soda water or so dangerous as joy-rides. What is more, the people's money, idle in their small pockets, creates a large taxable income in the treasure chests of movie magnates. If I were a politician, I should stake my last throw on the slogan, 'Movies for revenue only.'

No, the chief trouble is that even the perfect motiphotophonograph *will* leave a little to be desired; and it is just that little which counts — 'the little more, and how much it is!' The fact is, movies are not drama. They come very near to being drama, about as near as the man who

64

missed the ferry by a few feet and hoped to make it in two jumps. Suppose a perfect machine that synchronizes speech and action in perfect reproduction, suppose another Booth in Hamlet or another Mrs. Siddons in Lady Macbeth — they simply can't be transmitted by a machine, however sublimated.

For what makes drama real, what makes the illusion complete, is the slight variation that comes with each performance. In general, the interpretation is the same, the tones of voice and the gestures are approximately the same one night as another; but there is never a complete, machinely perfect identity in tone and gesture. For one thing, twenty-four hours have elapsed; the actor is not literally quite the same person. For another, the speech (and with it the action) must be affected by the personality of the actor at the moment of utterance and by other circumstances (among them the mindedness of the audience) at any particular performance, never exactly identical with those of any other performance. 'What!' you cry; 'call a thing that has its ups and downs, that is only once at its best (perhaps the night you are not there) superior to one that is crystallized forever on an invariable film?' Yes, that is what I have been trying to say. Great variation, mere irregularity, is dreadful; absolute invariability is possibly worse. For the element of variety, in itself a form of human reality, is part of the illusion, helps to make the art, the likeness to truth. Uniformity is an invention, not a creation. The movie star must remain a mimic, unresponsive to his audience. The actor, casting the spell of his human voice divine over his audience, may catch their rapture in return, give it back and receive it again, till he is lifted wholly into his part, till for one perfect moment he is exalted so that the likeness to truth of his performance, as by a miracle, becomes truth itself. And truth cannot be photographed — except on the sensitive film of the human spirit.

I make no special plea for singing, in which the human voice comes nearest to its divinity. I don't mean, of course, that I agree with my friend Exacticus, who holds that only the gifted should sing and that everybody else should be fined for singing. Quite the contrary, I think that everybody should sing, and I feel that those who can't (like myself) and those who won't (like Exacticus) should be treated with profound suspicion. In fact, I'm not sure that we shouldn't fine all who don't sing. Walt heard America singing, he said. I confess that I don't, though I hear plenty of noise. Sometimes I feel like the man in 'The King of Boyville' who said to Piggy Pennington, howling out a 'doleful ballad' — 'Well, son, wouldn't you just as lief sing as to make that noise?' But I wish America *would* sing. The will to sing is a great quality in a nation. Singing liberates poor inhibited souls; it ought to be encouraged if it is still alive.

Nevertheless, the art of singing well needs no apology. It is so rare and so marvelous that it will always compel admiration. The spoken word, rather, is what suffers the taint of mediocrity; or even, in the 'silent drama,' the ignominy of sheer obliteration. What wonder that we degenerate into monosyllabic grunts! Our priceless inheritance, the thing which might save us most surely from bestial oblivion, we have sold for a mess of machinery.

But there is no good in railing at the movies. Teach the children to speak and appreciate the values of speech; let them grow into human beings who realize that mind communicates to mind not merely through words but through tone of voice, through words given life and significance; treat dramatics and voice training not as an 'extra' but as an important part of the school work — the next generation will do the rest. 'Better Speech Week' may have its virtues. What we need, though, is a Better Speech Decade.

IN LOCO MAGISTRI

SOME years ago I heard a proud parent say sententiously that the chief educational institution should be the home.

'You mean,' I queried anxiously, 'that Papa should be a sort of head master?'

'Why, yes,' he replied with easy confidence. 'That is, in the deepest sense of the word. If you do the right thing by your children, provide the right sort of home and all that, it doesn't matter much what sort of school you send them to.'

The logic of these remarks, so far as they were intelligible, naturally appealed to a pedestrian mind. It is true enough that the child had to get his education at home before schools were ever thought of; and it is equally true that education should exist for the child, not for the school — though you might think, from the way some people talk, that education was a device invented to justify the existence of schools. It is only a perverse and complicated civilization that makes schools necessary at all. Furthermore, if it were not sweetly reasonable to believe that the parent is the child's chief teacher, the unrelenting mathematics of the situation would break down any pretension to the contrary. Conscienceless parent,

68

do you realize that your child is at school only one sixth of its waking hours? Less, even, if it has a normal predisposition to truancy!

Convincing enough, all this; but it was very discouraging to me. I felt that my wife, in spite of my hindrance, might approximate the 'right sort of home' stipulated by the aforesaid prophet; but I was worried by the 'all that' part of the prescription. The 'right sort of home' would be largely atmospheric, clearly the wife's province; but mysterious 'all that' — it must be no less a thing than the solemn business of education itself, clearly the obligation of Papa. Having just indulged rather heartily the hope that the school would accomplish with my children what I had utterly failed to do, having been told frequently that a good school ought to stand *in loco parentis* — I now realized, if this prophet was right, that it was I, not the school, who must stand *in loco parentis*. A curious dilemma for a *parent!*

It at once became a feverish necessity to find out what education was. Before long I discovered a good many people, both professional and amateur, ready to tell me all about it. Most of them reminded me of the man who said, 'I'm not argufyin'; I'm just a-tellin' you.' So I turned to books. But I found they said about the same things, though with a more artful pretense of argument. They used a good deal of technical language and said a

69

good many things I could not understand, so perhaps my conclusions aren't worth much; but I discovered, after a good deal of mental chewing, that such of their multifarious views as I could digest might be reduced to sixteen theories — eight looking one way, eight the other. Just how these antagonistic theories might be harmonized I did not see, and no one tried very hard to tell me; just what might become of the child ('vile body' under the educational scalpel) while we were experimenting, I did not like to think. For example: 'Education should allow greater freedom, that the child may realize its true self; beware of repression.' (But mine are not angelic little dears! It may be all right for them to 'realize their true selves' in a public school, but not in a decent, private house. At least, not twice!) *Per contra:* 'The secret is constant discipline; "spare the rod and spoil the child" is unpopular doctrine to-day, but it is *figuratively* as true as it ever was.' (Gargantuan grimace by the reader, I hope.)

But I won't weary you, dear reader (perhaps also a perplexed parent with a newly awakened conscience) — I won't list for you all sixteen of the theories, especially as some of them require graphs and charts, and others prove conclusively that your child and his father-before-him are 'low-grade morons.' Theories I call them, in my audacity. 'Fundamental principles' their champions

call them, in their humility. It is true that I
thought for a while that I might try them on alter-
nate days — bringing out the child's nature in all
its naked loveliness on Sunday, say, and beating
the devil out of the 'intolerable being' on Monday.
If one theory was right, I should find out in the
course of a year or so which it was. I might comfort myself somewhat, as I patched up my dis-
membered child, by thinking that I was doing a
great service to mankind. The adventure appealed to me — if only some one would lend me
his child.

Then, one day when I was wandering about,
the miserablest man in the whole town, I chanced
upon a friend who solved the riddle.

'Why,' he asked, when I unfolded to him my
melancholy dilemma, 'why believe any of them?'

To be sure, why? If they are so wholly at vari-
ance and so dogmatic, no one theory can be right.
I had now learned, as my friend went on to explain
with delightful assurance, what education was not.
In course of time, he added, I might learn what it
was — a practice not a theory.

That was *my* parental-magisterial fire-baptism,
my 'Everlasting No.' Thereafter I was free of
educational theory and, like Carlyle to his devil in
Leith Walk, could cry, 'I forever hate thee!' Possibly, if the child showed symptoms of loveliness, I
attempted to draw them out and told him that he

71

took after his father. Sometimes, perhaps, I recognized him as an 'intolerable being' and suited the action to the word. But I did these things only incidentally, with no reference in my mind to the sixteen theories; and I did a good many things not provided for by the orthodox rules.

What I did accomplish, though, was to find myself somewhat deeply *in loco magistri*. And the deeper I got in, the more I came to appreciate Kit Morley's fine saying, that teaching is 'a great and laborious art.' The more, too, I came to feel that I was right, as a teacher-*artist*, in not paying too *scientific* heed to the formulated theories. Indeed, of all the wise sayings I encountered in my search for the secret of education, only half a dozen have stood the test of practice in my slight experience. They admit of synthesis, too, if you want to get scientific about it; though I prefer to mumble them as a sort of educational *credo*:

First, 'Education does not generate or infuse a new principle; it only guides and directs a principle already in existence.' (The wisdom of Socrates.)

Second, Kit Morley's saying, quoted above, that teaching is 'a great and laborious art.'

Third, a favorite remark of a friend, a teacher of the old school: 'It takes two to make a teach.'

Fourth, from the late Samuel Thurber: 'Each teacher must make his own methods with his own wits.'

Fifth, from R. L. S.: 'The first step for all is to learn to the dregs our own ignoble fallibility.'

Sixth, a passing but pregnant phrase in a letter by a great head master, James Croswell: 'education, handing on the torch — a sacramental office '

This business of education, after all, is not a pathological problem, to be left wholly to specialists; it's the chief job of parents — perhaps the only justification they have left. And since the school has paraded itself as *in loco parentis* and has been fairly busy telling parents just what their job is, it seems reasonable that parents, *in loco magistri*, should have an opinion or two about the job of the school. Let's not be dictatorial about it; let's put it in the form of a question. If our schools and colleges are going to justify their calling to a 'sacramental office,' don't they need to take a vacation from the *abracadabra* of student-hours and courses by foot-pounds, and to pay more heed to what Bacon called the 'manurance of minds'?

Of course there may be an esoteric reason for *abracadabra*, which only the initiated can understand. But the schools and colleges will retort, I fear, that the reason is quite exoteric — simply the pressure of stupid and ignorant parents. 'You insist that your dear children shall go through this mummery, you believe, in your ignorance, that a mysterious virtue inheres in a college education for every boy and girl, you set foolish store by the "social value" of a degree; then you pay handsomely to support your curious faith and organize

73

your alumni associations to enforce it — what are we to do? We give you what you really want.'

So there is a 'both — and' aspect to this matter, too. It cuts both ways. The more I ponder the educational question, the more I feel that it is important for parents to find themselves *in loco magistri*; partly because it is their duty as well as their right, but also because they may then learn something about the schools and colleges. Instead of asking for more education, they may learn to ask for better education.

BULLS, BEARS, AND BEES

ABOUT the best thing Dan Chaucer ever wrote was the line which tells what he was accustomed to do when the month of May was come —

'Farewel my boke and my devocion.'

Only I should have gone him one better and have put *April* for *May* — hang the meter! He evidently felt much as I do, witness the famous lines at the beginning of his 'Canterbury Tales,' but I suppose he did not have modern facilities for hanging meter.

April sets the blood tingling. Bears, organgrinders, crocuses, and such things come out of their winter quarters. Bees cease the aimless flying that any warm day in winter puts them up to and begin to fly with a purpose and to hum a new tune. Bulls patrol the upland pastures. Civilization with its steam heat and artificial sunshine cannot wean us from the strange stirrings that transfigure man and beast and root at this magic season. The feet of the young men must be moving now — and woe to him who turns back to double over his crabbed book. Within, he must have recourse to potent spells to keep his spirits up; but if he goes forth, 'the implements of bliss are few' — a pair of stout shoes and the high heart of youth.

As for the three signs which I have chosen, in my title, as significant of spring, I confess to a rather extensive experience of bees and bulls. Bears I should hardly have included if the financial columns had not got me into the way of thinking that they were the inevitable reverse-picture of bulls. That is, a bull seen after a bad night is a bear, or a bear looked at between your legs becomes a bull. In the stock market the association of these two creatures, I am told, is of ancient origin; and the most credible explanation seems to be that bulls toss things up with their horns whereas bears pull things down with their paws. But the two beasts, as they roam about on 'change, have acquired far more distinctive characteristics than this. The 'bear' is crafty, with a kind of worldly-wise grouch. The 'bull,' on the other hand, is an optimistic, enthusiastic creature; though your professional 'bull' is of course playing a part — artfully pretending optimism so that you may catch the contagion and continue sick after he gets well.

No comparison with the real animals could be more inept, unless that which long ago wished Satanic character upon the poor serpent or in later times invented the 'venomous' toad. From what naturalist friends tell me, I should say bears were good-natured as a rule, much given to drowsiness, savage at times, but not grouchy, and almost the

76

least crafty of beasts. And I know that the bull is everything his prototype of the stock exchange is not.

The outstanding trait of your bull is sullenness. He may rage and imagine you a vain thing, but he bears *you* no particular grudge; he rages, not because of you, but because of his pervasive sullenness, his predetermined will to rage. Could you be miraculously removed from his course and another vile body substituted in your stead, he would still charge sullenly on. Your wayside dog is various and always interesting, whether as friend or foe. There is variety even in skunks. But the only difference I have been able to discern in bulls is the degree of their sullenness.

A bull or a bear in the stock market is an absurdity, when you come to think of it. Not all animals have been so grossly transmogrified in our imaginations. The favorites of beast epic and fable still run true to form — the crafty but suspicious fox, the self-sufficient cat, the friendly but carnivorous dog, the vain and uxorious cock. But thanks to dear old Isaac Watts and Maurice Maeterlinck, we are pretty well committed to a false picture of the bee.

Not that the bee is not busy — at times. Barring such incredible places as Southern California, where the bee works overtime while the humans do the heavy looking-on, it is busy more or less through six months of the year; and for a few weeks during the 'honey-flow' it is so deliriously busy that the New York Subway at rush hour, by comparison, seems as leisurely as an Old Man's Home. But the bee born in early summer never gets as far as the honey-flow of the following June. It putters about the place, gets a touch of work-fever when goldenrod is in bloom, and usually perishes with the early frosts. And the fellow (euphemism for lady-worker) born in the late summer has only played at working before the cold shuts down; then she huddles through the winter and spends her old age, in the spring, nursing the young athletes who are to riot in the clover fields. It may be all right for a bee, this life, but what should we think of our neighbors if they huddled for six months or if their young folk worked themselves to death in a few weeks?

Now I am quite aware that I am flying in the face of entrenched superstition. But any bee-keeper knows, or can know, if he takes the trouble to watch his bees closely, that a lot of flying and buzzing isn't work, that some bees work harder than others, and that colonies vary enormously in their capacity for labor. Once I sprinkled flour on a bee and watched its comings and goings. For the first couple of hours of a fine May morning it didn't go anywhere; it just flew about, lighted, went in and chatted in the hall with its friends, came out again and took the air, and then did it all over again. When it did get started, it stayed away for some time on each trip. I suppose it worked, for it came back laden and spent several minutes inside disposing of its load. This it kept up till about sundown, when it resumed the porch-gossip manner. A fair day's work, but rather less than a farmer has to put in at the same season.

Then there's that fellow Maeterlinck, who tells us enthusiastically of the perfect organization of the colony — every one in her proper place work-ing for the good of the whole, each worn-out worker going off to die when her work is done so that there is no need of undertakers; idle, noisy drones told exactly where they get off; all lady-workers loyal, dedicated, indefatigable. It's a pretty picture; but there is a touch of dull uni-formity, of self-sufficiency, and of inhospitality (not to say of stark Feminism) which is not even romantic when conceived in human terms. If we must have romance about bees, I favor the Pliny variety — for example: 'When foraging bees are overtaken in their expeditions by nightfall, they place themselves on their backs on the ground, to protect their wings from the dew, thus lying and watching until the first sign of dawn.'

Far be it from me to shock the nature-lovers. But I don't mind shocking the nature-fakers. Nature, to my way of thinking, is more in-

79

teresting and instructive if we take her as she is.

We can certainly learn a lot from the bee. Not indeed the too obvious combination of Wall Street and Palm Beach, a combination of frenzied busyness and downright idleness which that old reprobate Watts translated into improvement of each shining hour; nor do we really find a model of social and civil perfection in the merciless, self-contained, cutthroat communities idealized by Maeterlinck. Imitating them is not our cue, any more than it is a happy thought to emulate the bull or the bear or the uxorious cock.

> 'It is not growing like a tree
> In bulk, doth make man better be.'

No, what virtue we derive from flora and fauna springs not from imitation of them (one seems to remember cabbage-headed delvers), but rather from quickened senses and steady ways of living. If you can't flutter at gardening, much less can you do so in the apiary. Perhaps the best thing Maeterlinck said in his 'Life of the Bee' was that the bee-keeper should use 'slow, large motions.' Not, indeed, because the bee does, but rather because it doesn't.

I recall the first time I learned the virtue of slow, large motions — from an old bee-keeper who was initiating me into the mysteries of apiculture. He was a sentimental old cove, called his queen bee 'Prosperina,' and had got hold of most of the superstitions, including the model community idea. But he also believed and preached the doctrine of slow, large motions; and they had so far become second nature with him that an incredible tranquillity rested upon him.

At first I was a good deal alarmed by the buzzing (several thousand bees can make a tremendous noise); but he rebuked me gently, told me I must learn to distinguish this joyous hum from the snarl of angry bees.

'If I should inadvertently crush one with my thumb,' he went on, 'its cry of pain would immediately disturb the whole colony. *Then* you would hear them snarl!' He said this almost gleefully; then added: 'If that should happen, remember to go slowly; don't run and wave your arms. Go certainly, but go slowly.'

Before long the gentle old soul must have 'crushed one with his thumb,' for suddenly, in place of the 'joyous hum,' arose a new noise, multitudinous, menacing, an indubitable snarl. Before you could say Jack Robinson, a young privateer, her decks cleared for action, boarded my cheek and drove me from the bucolic scene.

The gentle apiarist put the frame back, closed the hive, and walked unscathed through a cloud of bees till he found me peeking out from behind a tree.

'You went certainly,' he said gently, 'but you know you didn't go slowly.'

THE CHILDREN OF THE WAY

A PEDESTRIAN may pretend that he passes bucolic days sprinkling flour on honey-bees or dodging bulls in the upland pastures, but even he cannot avoid the stern, mirthless facts which confront men and women in the crowded streets. Stopping on the brow of a hill and looking down on a distant, shimmering city, he may cry, 'How beautiful!' — but there is always that fellow at his shoulder to exclaim, 'Beautiful? How *earnest!*' And when he descends into the plain and walks in the city streets, where the celestial haze has turned to dirty smoke, and the soothing murmur has grown to a discordant din, he cannot wholly escape crying, like Ruskin, of 'the misery that I know of, and see signs of where I know it not, which no imagination can interpret too bitterly.'

It may be good to return to the hilltop, to see the distant, beautiful city as well as to echo the lamentations of Ruskin. It may be profitable to remember Turi the Lapp, who says he cannot think unless a stiff breeze is blowing through his hair. But no amount of persiflage or of bucolic gambol can blot out the picture and the noise. Those who have followed the Pedestrian hitherto in the pathetic expectation that he might eventually squeeze a jest out of the preposterous illusions of mankind are hereby warned to turn back. To-day he is concerned seriously, not with illusions, which are often funny things, but with disillusion, which is a bitter thing.

For the real misery, 'which no imagination can interpret too bitterly,' is not the condition of the poor, nor yet, except in a secondary sense, what Ruskin called the 'deforming mechanism' of modern life. Rather, it is widespread disillusion, especially among the young, and a pathetic clutching at spiritual nostrums and anodynes. Perhaps most youthful ideals are illusions, but when disillusionment came slowly and in part, you could build new and less hollow illusions out of the ruins of the old, and eventually, out of these, could build still less illusory faiths, till ideals settled into something like reality, till you saved, or felt that you were in process of saving, your 'crown of spiritual manhood.'

But Youth still abhors a vacuum. So our dis-enchanted youth are feverishly busy trying to find a way out. Of course the young pagans, noisy and conspicuous, are really a negligible minority, in spite of the apprehensions of serious middle-aged folk; and they are certainly franker and possibly more engaging as giddy satyrs and giddier satyr-esses than when, formerly, they hardened slowly into swine. And they are happy enough — as long

83

as youth lasts! But a multitude of young people are unhappy just because they are *not* materialists. Marriage and social relations, work and play, politics and religion — their suddenly opened eyes see these things in a kind of bankruptcy. They would not only save their own souls, they would save the whole world. And they realize at least this much, that the solution lies not in material, but in spiritual power. They are turning to religion for a way out.

This is of course an encouraging sign. But it would be more encouraging if they did not seize so passionately on devices which only breed further disillusionment. Perhaps it is the fault of their elders, who seem almost as hysterically bent on finding a device, a get-saved-quick solution. Some, of an emotional nature, mistake psychic forces for spiritual; others imagine that they can think the mystery through, as if it were a problem. Perhaps the most numerous are the thralls of efficiency, who suppose that organization will work miracles. Only the other day the newspaper heading for a prominent clergyman's solution of the European tangle was 'Christianity Must Organize for Assurance of World Peace.'

The article wasn't so bad as the title. It was mainly concerned with the reasonable idea that statesmen, actuated by Christian motives, should work towards an association of nations. But the

author did talk glibly of *organizing* Christianity
itself. Just a careless use of terms on his part,
perhaps, but a very different matter to the disillusioned who clutch at the idea. Yet it is a com-
monplace, tantalizing equally to the methodical or
to the sentimental mind, that what we do to regulate spiritual things usually kills them. At least
the most striking instances of creative Christianity
have taken place without organization. One vivid
illustration, among many, is in 'The Children of
the Way,' by Anne Allinson.

This little book gives an extraordinarily convincing picture of the positive and miraculous
grace of early Christianity. The author is so inti-
mate with Imperial Rome that she accomplishes
an astonishing likeness to fact. You feel as if you
were literally there, in the Argiletum, or at Dento's
pearl shop in the Via Sacra, or in the *atrium* of the
house of the Good Shepherd; yet Mrs. Allinson
has given her characters such perennial life and
has selected her situations with such skill that the
whole thing might be translated without much effort to our own day. You read of the careless,
riotous throng at the Circus or of the festivities at
a tavern in the Subura, and your mind instinc-
tively leaps forward to that startling phrase of
Henry Adams — 'the age-long failure of Christianity roaring up out of Broadway.' The dejected
laborer contemplating suicide as he looks down at

85

the Tiber might be standing on Brooklyn Bridge or the Victoria Embankment; the scene in the servants' hall might be 'below stairs' in Fifth Avenue or Grosvenor Square; Calpurnius and Felicia, a young patrician couple riding for a divorce, might be anywhere west of Constantinople. Yet they are all vividly, poignantly, in the Rome of Nero — a disillusioned Rome, in which a noble but sadly sterile Stoicism offered only 'close-lipped patience' to the spiritually sick.

In the last chapter Honoria, an independent, intellectual woman, writes to her brother in Egypt of her visit to Paul in prison. 'As we talked on,' she says, 'I saw that much that these Christians teach is old and familiar.' Then, near the end of her letter: 'But I think that they live it (the littlest sort of everyday life) in the presence of God and of eternity. I am aware that philosophers have preached some such sort of abstraction as this, but I must confess to you that I have never in my whole life seen one individual, not even Mother, who was doing it as these Christians are. They seem set free from every inhibition.'

What strikes you most in the book, in fact, is not the vivid way in which it is written, but the remarkably vital power of a few poor people, with no organization, with ignorance, indifference, and persecution confronting them, but with the grace of God in their hearts — 'set free from every inhibition.' And reflecting on the spiritual impotence and the inhibitions which organized Christianity has set up through the centuries, you are inclined to wonder whether the secret of the Children of the Way did not lie, after all, in their very lack of organization; to wonder, indeed, whether the 'Way' is not the 'way out.'

Organization is a characteristic of what we commonly regard as civilization. It must therefore be a disquieting thought to some that the 'Way' of the 'Children' might wreck civilization, the very thing the organizers would seek to save. One is reminded of a reply said to have been made by Bishop Brent to a similar objection at the outbreak of the World War. 'Well,' said a shortsighted person to him, 'this war proves one thing: Christianity's a failure; Civilization and Christianity cannot get on together.'

'If that's the case,' Bishop Brent replied, with quick lucidity, 'then Civilization will have to go.'

PEGASUS AND TAXICABS

THE Editor, making an Archibald Henderson
face, asked me the other day what a pedestrian thought of poetry. Picking up the cue with
Shavian grace, I was tempted to say, like the man
from Chicago to the man from Boston, 'I don't
think of it.' Possibly I did say (with the old Shaw
in me struggling to put on a new Chesterton) that
poetry nowadays is on the one hand a ghostly
parody of itself and on the other a grotesque
posture.

But most of these bitter things a pedestrian says
falsely. It is your flivver mind which discerns only
two roads and which, on finding one blocked for
repairs, bumps incontinently down the other; that
kind of mind assumes of course that posturing is
the only alternative to an echo. There is a great
deal of real poetry being made nowadays. You
cannot wander down the highways and byways
without noticing it.

Not that I am particularly qualified to talk
about it. In my flivverous youth perchance I mistook the cacophony of valves for the sweet whirring of the wings of Pegasus. We all suppose, at
one time or another, that a taxicab will fly if only
we rent it from a certain garage in Moorfields,

kept by the father of John Keats. Still, they say that critics are artists who have failed. (Editor: 'Pox! Leave thy damnable faces and begin!') All right, Mr. Editor, let's draw up to the fire and talk about this poetry, which, whatever we think of it, is being written and read with a fervor that it has not enjoyed these hundred years.

Every one knows that poetry took a new lease of life about fifteen years ago. Ten years before that you could count on the fingers of one hand (three fingers lacking) the poets who were making headway with the public: Kipling, because he refused to follow the word-mongers and because he struck a new vein which appealed to 'men in a world of men'; Ella Wheeler Wilcox, because she knew how to reach the multitude who take poetry as I do afternoon tea — weak and no lemon. Most of the great Victorians were dead or silent. Swinburne, Meredith (as a poet), and Yeats were read only by college youth and a handful of devotees; Hardy was still looked on as a novelist; Stephen Phillips had an exaggerated but only temporary vogue. Such younger writers as were producing robustly in traditional rhythms (I think particularly of William Vaughn Moody) found an astonishingly indifferent public. Then, almost as at the stroke of a magician's wand (perhaps the magician was in the Poetry Book-Shop in London), poets began to be heard. Masefield and Noyes and Newbolt, who had been writing for some time, came into their own; 'The Shropshire Lad' was discovered; before long, Robinson, Frost, and Amy Lowell, as well as scores of younger writers, headed by the imperishable names of Rupert Brooke and Alan Seeger, went into edition after edition. Poetry societies, poetry magazines, poets discussed by competent critics — poetry taken seriously! Whence this sudden interest?

Of course your honest-to-goodness critic says that we live in a peculiarly poetic age, an age of youth, of vision, of creative impulse; and the inference is that the two decades from 1890 to 1910 were spiritually dead, crabbed, mean, unproductive of anything but material expansion. That may be partly true, but it is too glib to dismiss thus a period in which Stevenson had his greatest vogue and in which the modern drama came into being. The real reason probably lay, as Amy Lowell has pointed out, in the fact that poets, with few exceptions, had been mouthing outworn formulas and had not till recently awakened to the purposes and possibilities of poetry.

It is common to blame Keats for setting a pace none else could follow. It doesn't seem quite fair; it's something like blaming God, in the moral world, for a good fellow gone wrong. Still, perhaps little has done more harm to the cause of poetry than his famous lines about Beauty and Truth —

'that is all
Ye know on earth, and all ye need to know.'

All ye need to know in heaven perhaps! But *on
earth* the degenerate inheritors of the Keats tradition, with their own private conceptions of Truth
and Beauty, have merely shifted the counters
which represent Love and Spring Sunsets and have
supposed that they were writing poetry. First,
pictures: then blank negatives called pictures; —
the imagists have rightly recalled us to the 'exact
word.' But still only pictures (for *spoken* words):
Robert Frost has rightly recalled us to 'tones of
voice.' Certainly poets are awakening to a new
realization of their art.

But not *all* poets! Nor the reading public. A
good many people are only half awake — still rub-
bing their eyes. But that needn't dismay us.
There is always a period of dislocation between
fashions, in poetry as in religion, when the champions of the Auld Kirk look on the advocates of the
New as frivolous heretics; while the new folk, in
rejecting the prejudices of the old, blithely throw
overboard most of the principles too. We seem
recently to have been in some such state, though
latterly we are beginning to see a little out of one
eye and to snatch back some of the Victorian
virtues we had so wantonly jettisoned.

In the nineteenth century the notion flourished
that a strong feeling, mouthed in cosmic phrase,

was the real thing (contemptuous grimace toward Pope and the pumiced phrase). Recently, in our own day, harsh realism and disdain of tradition have set up another fashion, the fashion of difference (contemptuous grimace toward Tennyson and the cosmic phrase). The extremists have done us a great service, though; particularly the imagists; they have slipped the trammels of exigent meter and fatuous rhyme; they have called us back to the important principle that images must be 'hard and clear.' But, like their predecessors, they have become somewhat entoiled in the meshes of their own web. They are so afraid of being cosmic that they are often trivial; they are so afraid of tradition that they are often queer; they are so afraid of the expansive heart that they exalt the contracted mind. It is of course the extremists with no definite philosophy of poetry, with only the dogma of difference, who do the most conspicuous posturing. Andrew Lang, if he were fighting them to-day as he did when he wrote his fine outburst against 'the low lutes of love,' would find a different foe. He might have a fling, perhaps, at the strident saxophones of verse; and, instead of poetasters 'lulled by the song of Circe and her wine,' he might decry the votaries of 'dark-veiled Cotytto' — 'goddess of nocturnal sport.' But, although his condemnation would be different, he would recall us to the same truths now as then.

Poetry is still a creative art, not just an exquisite craft. There must still be the *creating word* — not merely the exact thing-word, but the thought-provoking image; not merely the logical word, but the 'analogical' word. Granted the word, moreover, there must still be the significant thought or feeling — in Pope's magnificent image the 'light' created by the word. Pope of course said it in satirical vein (he wore his rue with a difference) —

> 'Lo! thy dread empire, Chaos, is restored;
> Light dies before thy uncreating word.'

But we are beginning to realize, after a century of scoffing, why Dr. Johnson, hearing that Pope's voice had failed him when he repeated these lines, remarked, 'And well it might, sir, for they are noble lines.' Without 'light,' poetry may be pretty, it may be interesting; it may serve to decorate an otherwise unfurnished mind; but it can hardly transfigure thought. The 'creating' word must not merely arrest attention; it must focus and direct the imagination. It isn't the whole of poetry, to be sure; but I sometimes wonder whether it and the 'light' it creates aren't what our commercial friends call 'the priceless ingredient.'

Let me add that I'm interested to hear 'The Forum' is going to give poetry a conspicuous place in the magazine. That should encourage you, Mr. Editor, to select the best, in self-defense, instead of following the feeble custom of selecting harm-

93

less poetry to hide in the spaces below prose articles. For poetry is fire — which, if harmless, is ashes.

I trust you will reveal a catholic taste, sir. There is room in our hearts for humorous verse, for satirical verse, for Gargantuan grin, and for fairy frolic. I hope you will show your readers that free verse has its place: to give vivid pictures, to express incisive thoughts. But I hope you will show them, too, that only traditional rhythms, musically metrical, can carry a truly lyrical mood. Remember —

'Ay, thou poor ghost!' he cried, as he hurried out; but the rest of his answer was swallowed up by a great noise. Was it the whirring of the wings of Pegasus — or only a taxicab in low gear?

BUBS

'HELLO, BUB!'

Those of us who spent a happy boyhood in the past century recall the cheery greeting of the passing gent. We did not mind being called 'bubs.' Usually the natural stoicism of youth accepted the salutation with complete indifference. If we felt anything, though, we had a sneaking fondness for it. Certainly the gent who thus greeted us was less objectionable than the crusty old party who commanded sternly, 'No skylarking, boys.' *He* always got the snowball — if we dared. I'm not sure what the modern equivalent for 'bub' is. I always try 'Hello, Oliver,' and meet with sufficient success, especially if I follow it with a voluble question like 'How are your honorable insides this bright morning?' A boy likes an old dog that wags his tail.

But what was a bub? What are the amiable urchins whom I call Oliver? We know well enough that we were all different, quite separate individuals to ourselves; but obviously we were just happy boys, all alike, to the cheery gent; and naughty boys, all alike, to the crusty old party.

Perhaps it's more to the point to wonder what strange manner of man was the cheery gent — the undiscriminating creature who always called us bubs. For in the steady practice of his kindly greeting he seems to have tinctured his own character with something of the dull sameness he ascribed to us. Bubs indeed! We were different enough. He was the regular, dyed-in-the-wool, honest-to-goodness bub himself!

As long as bubs project their undiscriminating minds into their greeting of small boys, all honor to them. It may warm the heart of some urchin who so far forgets himself as to heed it. But one cannot avoid noticing that the habit of bubbing persists, so that some people apply it, without fear or favor, to all sorts and conditions of men and women. It is as though they said, 'If this be democracy, make the most of it.' But they don't really say that, or even think that. They are just bubs by instinct. So they go their glad way shouting, 'Hi, Bill,' to a man whom they have met only once and whose name happens to be Josiah; and they further satisfy their welling friendliness by adding a cheery 'How's the old girl?' — without indicating whether they refer to Josiah's hypothetical wife or to his deceased mother.

Well, why shouldn't they? Why isn't it cheery behavior? Surely, bubbery is better than snobbery. People actually take infection from the bub, or if they are immune, they at least admire him. They say he is a 'good mixer,' a 'jolly fellow.'

After all, 'he means well.' Alas, he doesn't *mean* at all; he just *is*.

In fact, if you stop to think about it, a bub isn't really the opposite of a snob. The opposite of a snob, as every one knows, is a Christian gentleman, 'in apprehension how like a god!' But your honest-to-goodness bub has no apprehensions; he is in truth a sort of inverted snob — not the converse of a snob, but what our mathematical enemies used to call the contrapositive. If a floorwalker should clap you on the shoulder, reader, and call you 'Brother,' he *might* be a snob, for he would no doubt be envious of your high estate. But when the next minute I come shuffling through the maze of shoppers and he treats me in the same cordial manner, he is a downright bub; his dull eyes cannot see the difference between the owner of a Rolls Royce and the owner of a pair of ground grippers. Far be it from me to decry the cheery spirit. If in gay courtesy he anticipated your thoughts with a happy remark about the slippery roads 'this icy weather,' and then turned to me with an equally happy 'Fine bracing air this morning, sir; yes, sir, bargain sale in the basement,' he would be crude, perhaps, but he would resemble a human being. But to wear the same face and to fling the same greeting to every one — no, it is not Christian charity on his part. He has no power of distinction. Not merely all coons, but all people look alike to him. In fact, the more you think about it, the more the snob takes on something almost akin to sanctity compared to his inverted brother. At least the snob's head is up; he sees and observes distinctions. But this other fellow, galumphing about on all fours, is a sad travesty of a man.

Bubbing is of course very common. America, I fear, has gone in for it on a colossal scale. Instead of a decent fear of being a bub, Mr. Man is in reality singularly eager to be one. He is convinced that no home is complete without a bub. France gave us the dandy; England produced the snob; Africa is responsible for the tsetse-fly; but, O my country, it remained for America to spawn the bub!

I have often thought that it might be an edifying exercise to consider the degrees and kinds of bubs. The ecclesiastical bub, thick as autumnal leaves, has come into his own in a 'socialized' church. The business bub never becomes president of a bank, but he meets with astonishing success in trade. In fact, the whole advertising business, seen aright, is a strange acrobatic blend of bubbery and snobbery. The kaleidoscopic gestures of Broadway — what do they really do but shout in one ear of the rustic philosopher, 'Climb aboard; there's always room for more,' while in the other ear they hiss, 'Heads I win;

tails you lose'? Innocent, cheery little lights they seem — to the bub. Then there are the university bubs ('Ra Ra Boys') and the traveling bubs, the golfing bubs, and the motor bubs, and, last but not least, the lady bubs. In fact, almost every class of human beings contains bubs except the one group of urchins to whom the term is commonly applied.

The scientific material on bubs is still very slight. Some day, perhaps, we shall be able to catalogue every variety with the accuracy they do not deserve. Meanwhile we can identify without much probability of error the *genus*, if not every *sub-species*. Speaking roughly, then, one may hazard the statement that vasty wildernesses and gardens are the only places where bubs do not abound. Of course it is not the arduous labor of gardening that deters them. A bub would hoe corn, would even ride the fords o' hell if by so doing he could be a greater, more conspicuous, more sublimely vacuous bub.

REFORM

BESIDES Exacticus there is one man at the club who still seems willing to talk to me. *To* rather than *with* — but how unlike Exacticus! This one develops beautiful theories, millennial visions, huge cloudy symbols of a high reform. If ever my back-yard gardening takes on Burbank pretensions and I invent a new flower, I shall name it after him: *Nebulosa rosea grandiflora*.

Yet, though he speaks often of reforms, I should hardly call him a typical reformer. There is a tenacity, an irrepressibility, about your dyed-in-the-wool reformer. He can advocate one reform in 1896 and, when he is repudiated, can go blithely on for forty years advocating repudiated reforms. Such a person does not believe in ideas; he believes in himself. Now my friend Nebulosa believes in ideas, but collapses utterly at the suggestion that he put them into practice; is honest enough, even, to say naïvely, 'I never thought of that,' when some one meets him with a counter-thrust.

At first glance it would appear that reformers may be divided into two classes: those who think and those who do. Thus you have your Rousseau and your Thoreau; your John Ruskin and your Jacob Riis. It is a very satisfactory classification, this of the dreamers and the doers, because it will fit almost any consideration of anything under the sun; and on that account it is wholly *un*satisfactory. The point is, not whether my friend Nebulosa is a dreamer while Snodgrass is a doer, but rather why they are both called 'reformers' — what, indeed, this business of reform is anyhow.

It is idle, I suppose, to worry about the origin of the word *reform*, even if a strayed European did innocently fancy that a reformer was a person who came from a reformatory. Words have shifty characters. There's *smell*, for example. One used to hear of the 'odor of sanctity,' but it would never have done to speak of the 'smell of sanctity' — even if sanctity should in all fitness 'smell to heaven.' So it will not do to worry too much about the fact that reform has nothing to do, as it ought to have, with reshaping old ways to new conditions. It appears to mean abolition, sometimes substitution. Our lexicographer gives this meaning as 'rare,' but it seems to be the usual sense of the word nowadays.

Here, at least, is a lead towards an honest classification. We may not expect reformers to do anything so literal as to reshape good things that have fallen to decay, but we may reasonably ask them to give us a substitute better than the original. Alas, some of them, whether dreamers or doers, seem bent only on a difference — occasionally,

even, on a *deform* rather than a *reform*. It is quite
necessary, in fact, to bear constantly in mind that
reform has nothing whatever to do with reform;
then we shall more readily understand and ap-
praise the reformer — deformer, transformer,
whatever you choose to call him; — in any event a
militant figure, with these three striking characteristics: a conviction that because he wants
to have his way he ought to have his way; a mysterious notion that he is a practical man; and no
longer of 'meagre face deform' (the humorous
weeklies are sadly out of date in this matter), but
of full-blooded, sanguine visage. So equipped, he
is invincible. Charles Lamb's retort to the impu-
dent fellow who roared at him, 'I pride myself,
sir, on being a matter-of-fact man,' though just,
is of no avail. 'And I pride myself,' said Lamb,
'on being a matter-of-lie man.' Lamb's world is
in the discard; the reformer holds all the tricks.

It may seem a melancholy reflection, that the
reformer has so little to do with real reform, but it
is really an enheartening thought if we stick to it.
For it not only gives us a basis for honest classification, but once we know him for what he is, we
may find a vermicide for him too. A distinguished
Scot, after a considerable residence in this country, has come to the conclusion that the chief characteristic of America is that half the people want to
organize and that the other half want to be or-

ganized. Here, then, is the adequate classification. It takes two to make a reform; the reformee is just as much a party to the crime as the reformer. Stevenson wrote that 'it is this itch of doing that undoes men'; but if he had been living in America to-day, it would have been necessary to add, 'It is this itch of being done that undoes men.'

The wonder is, with all this itching, that the vast practice of reform hasn't been put on a legal basis, like any other profession. Why not a State examination, after an appropriate period at a reform school (new style), and a license which could be framed and placed conspicuously in the practitioner's shop? (I should like to draw up the curriculum for that school, and to apply for the office of Dean. Breaking stones for an hour would be a 'prerequisite' for breakfast, and above the pile of stones would be the solemn sign, 'You can't get something for nothing.') Then the reformees would know who the licensed practitioners were, and any reformers who dared to practice without a license could be hustled into a reform school (old style).

For this business of reform, like automobiles and painless dentistry, has come to stay. It is fatuous to imagine that we can put the busybodies out of business by exterminating the reformees. All that we can hope is to do something

toward reclaiming a good word, something towards reshaping a broken world by insisting on a
license (a high license, of course, for 'high reforms')
and by taking care ourselves to eschew the itch
of being done.

Personally, I incline to favor my friend Nebulosa, the reformer who is not a 'reformer,' the man
who has more faith in ideas than he has in himself.
I should give him an honorary degree. And if ever
there should come a day when we put our reformers in cages and breed a special race of reformees
for their diet, we must remember to build a university for our Nebulosæ — our inglorious, if not
wholly mute, Miltons and Wordsworths and
Emersons. For sometimes they 'dream true'; and
when they do, reform is worthy of its name. A
plague on your reforms that can be encompassed
by legislation! But honor to the dreams which
'set the standard of humanity some furlongs forward into chaos!'

THE INELUCTABLE SPRING

WHEN any one says 'weather' in New England, it is the cue for a jest. To Pilgrim Fathers, confronted with the thing itself rather than with careless conversation about it, it was no doubt a bitter jest. But to your modern, except perhaps when there is a coal strike on, it is always cause for humorous comment. I know one man, to be sure, who says he is too busy to notice the weather; but his ancestors came from Cape Cod, so he is probably jesting too; he means that the weather is too busy to notice him. Then there is the old lady who says, 'Don't talk to me about the weather!' You understand, of course, that she really wants you to talk about it; she is on the perilous edge of temperament and relishes the danger.

In New England everybody talks about the weather, even though, as Mark Twain pointed out, 'Nobody seems to do anything about it.' There is no question that a merry New-Englander with a large balance of Puritan sobriety to live down can make up for his ancestors by diligent attention to meteorology. I once knew a melancholy wag who, looking out on a particularly mean morning, was wont to say solemnly, 'This day I devote to rum.' Charles Dudley Warner's comments on the weather used to be famous, but are now, alas, strangely unknown. Yet he was the Shakespeare of meteorologists. Hear him, the father of all columnists, on 'How Spring Came in New England':

> The first day there is slush with rain; the second day, wind with hail; the third day, a flood with sunshine. . . . Man shivers and sneezes. . . . This is called the breaking-up of Winter. . . . Nature, in fact, still hesitates, puts forth one hepatica at a time, and waits to see the result; pushes up the grass slowly, perhaps draws it in at night. This indecision we call Spring.

Most of the jesters and gentle cynics concentrate on spring. The weather, Mark Twain says, 'gets through more business in spring than in any other season. In the spring I have counted one hundred thirty-six different kinds of weather within four and twenty hours. It was I who made the fame and fortune of the man who had that marvelous collection of weather on exhibition at the Centennial. . . . He was going to travel around the world and get specimens from all climes. I said, "Don't do it; just come to New England on a favorable spring day."' It was Lowell, wasn't it, who wrote, 'May's so awfully like Mayn't'? And it was in the spring that Warner discovered the thirteenth wind. All the twelve winds of heaven blow at any season, but it is in

March and April that Warner's 'Zenith Wind' gets in its playful work. Boston is incontestably the meteorological center of the 'roaring forties.'

Of course most of the serious literature about New England weather is absurd. It is bookish, full of English tradition — April showers, May Day, and things which are not New English. Take the familiar saying about March coming in like a lion or a lamb. It usually comes in like the composite monster that John Mandeville saw — a 'boar-headed, bear-bodied, lion-tailed, six-legged beast.' This year it came in like a yellow dog. Then it went out like a whole menagerie. In fact, among all the weather jingles, I can find only one that holds true in New England:

> 'Sunset at night, sailor's delight;
> Sunset in the morning, sailors take warning.'

Even the honest-to-goodness poets borrow properties for their pictures of New England spring. Emerson, to be sure, wrote of a 'tumultuous privacy of storm' as if he knew what he was talking about; but he appears to have had winter in mind. Bryant, ecstatic in his memory of Cummington springs, gives us real New England birds — the cheery bobolink not least. And one remembers gratefully Henry van Dyke's 'Veery.' But the trouble is, most spring poets find the weather always fair, and that simply isn't New England.

107

There was one New England poet, though, who saw the other side. Emily Dickinson recorded all kinds of weather. If she wrote,

> 'The hills untied their bonnets,
> The bobolinks begun,'

and

> 'The mornings blossom into noons
> And split their pods of flame,'

she wrote also:

> 'A narrow wind complains all day
> How some one treated him;
> Nature, like us, is sometimes caught
> Without her diadem.'

What is more to the point, she recorded it because she saw its significance. The trouble with the jesters is that they are so near the facts of New England spring that they miss the truth of it. The poets, who sometimes miss the facts, are nearer the truth. The springtime, after all, even New England springtime, is 'a glorious birth.' Emily Dickinson was nearest of all to the truth, for she knew both the facts and their significance.

To her spring was not the pretty sight of a shy maiden scattering flowers; nor the steady vision of an unconquerable warrior putting the rear guard of winter to rout. These are romantic fancies; they may represent a natural process in some unfavored spot. But true spring, like life itself, is not regenerate all at once. The old Adam lingers; there are set-backs and failures, throes and a struggle, before the final triumph.

Perhaps there is no virtue in cussedness, for its own sake, but in weather it makes a fine foil to blessedness. At least, I observe that the people who revile New England weather and seek out perfect climates return sooner or later if they can and 'put up' with the weather. Why, bless you, they love it! Their instinct is sure; it is merely their diagnosis that is wrong. Sub-tropical winter, after all, is an anodyne; March in New England is a tonic.

As I write, the ice of last evening has vanished miraculously from the trees, the slush in the roads has turned to mud, the steaming fields are calling to the plough, and the meadow-larks, half sad, half jubilant, like proper Puritan birds, are singing in a doubtful spring. They, poor things, know that the morrow may come shrouded in snow; but the thoughtless human, looking out on a perfect day, has no doubt that the season of joy and gladness is at hand. And when, a few minutes later, an ugly wind gets up and plays its 'old measure in the boughs,' he is sure of it. These are the throes.

No, it isn't the bobolink or the veery that signalizes spring. When they are at their best, you are on the threshold of summer. Then come sultry days and fitful winds, and June bugs and cut worms and mosquitoes and summer tourists. The

song sparrow and the meadow-lark are your true
spring birds in New England — singing in the gale
that works in the barren branches. That is the
tune of spring in New England; that is the tune to
which our sturdy forefathers marched forth with
vigor, to subdue a fertile but stubborn soil. Hear
Emily sing it — she has the key:

> 'Of all the sounds despatched abroad,
> There's not a charge to me
> Like that old measure in the boughs,
> That phraseless melody
>
> 'The wind does, working like a hand
> Whose fingers brush the sky,
> Then quiver down, with tufts of tune
> Permitted gods and me.
>
> 'When winds go round and round in bands,
> And thrum upon the door,
> And birds take places overhead,
> To bear them orchestra,
>
> 'I crave him grace, of summer boughs,
> If such an outcast be,
> He never heard that fleshless chant
> Rise solemn in the tree,
>
> 'As if some caravan of sound
> On deserts, in the sky,
> Had broken rank, then knit, and passed
> In seamless company.'

CAPE COD HUMOR

ONCE, when I had so far abandoned my pedestrian convictions as to accept a lift in a flivver (compassionate reader, it was a hot, sandy road in New Jersey), I noticed that the driver leaned overboard and looked past the wind-shield. In fact, he couldn't see *through* it, it was so dirty.

'The sun on that glass,' I remarked sympathetically, 'makes it difficult to see, doesn't it?'

'Well,' replied the driver, with no suggestion of mirth in his tone, 'you kin almost see through it. I'll have to give it a coat o' paint pretty soon.'

The pronunciation betrayed him, to be sure, as did his lean, weather-beaten face, but I think it was the type of his jest that chiefly prompted my next question. 'You come from Cape Cod?' I queried.

'Not far from there,' he answered matter-of-factly. 'Born and brought up in Falmouth.'

Every serious reading-circle comes, sooner or later, to a debate in regard to wit and humor. It never seems to occur to the debaters that you might as well try to define poetry or generosity as to attempt to label humor in general. Only in its specific manifestations can it be ticketed. You

may describe dramatic poetry or Robinson's generosity with some accuracy; and just so you may
approximate a label for Scotch humor, or Cockney
humor, or Cape Cod humor. But though the sum
of different kinds of poetry or of different degrees
of generosity may give you a rough idea of poetry
or of generosity, you have to recognize, with the
sad example of the debating club before you, that
the sum of all the particular kinds of humor will
not add up to a definition of the abstract quality,
Humor. That is perhaps the most humorous thing
about humor; its expressions are so concrete; it,
itself, is so uncapturably abstract. We offer, therefore, no encouragement whatever to the debating
societies; we are concerned with specific manifestations.

Now the most obvious thing about Cape Cod
humor (*pace* Chesterton) is that it is humorous
because it isn't humorous. It may have much in
common with other New England varieties, but
it has two particular differences. Most New England humor of the 'dry' variety emerges in an in-
congruous seriousness; in fact, it takes its life from
that seriousness. But generally it betrays, by a
twinkle of the eye or a peculiar emphasis, that it
is not meant to be taken in absolute earnest. You,
the listener, are given a chance to share in the suppressed merriment. But your Cape Cod humorist
never vouchsafes a sign. To do so would be to

deny his nature and to spoil the jest. The merriment is so wholly suppressed that it is not only inaudible, but absolutely invisible.

The other particular difference is that, whereas most humor is made partly for some one else's benefit, Cape Cod humor is made solely for the maker's delight. In fact, much of it depends on its not being recognized. You are never asked to share; you are not even given a chance. You must *take* a share. If you do so in the right way, you may almost please the originator (vanity reaches even to Chatham Bars) — but you mustn't laugh; you must answer in kind — a trifle drier if possible. The true Cape native will then show his delight by making no sign whatever. If he should laugh, it would be out of politeness; he would recognize for your sake that you thought you were making a joke. Only uproarious silence signifies perfect *rapport*.

The prime quality, then, is seriousness exaggerated to an absolute point, complete suppression of any sign of intended mirth. If my friend of the flivver had changed his tone in the slightest, if he had stressed the word 'almost' or 'see' never so little, the joke might have been a good one from Hartford east to Maine, but not from New Bedford to Harwichport.

I remember, for example, a story of a Vermonter's humor.

'What,' he cried, 'you never saw Mrs. Smith? Well, she was Hen Smith's wife, and of all the ugly, ornery-lookin' wimmin, she took the cake. Why, whenever the conductor wanted to lead a train by their house, he had to ask Hen to call her in off the veranda.' Then after a pause: 'Well, I s'pose, ef you went fer enough back in hist'ry, you might find she was descended from the human race, but there warn't no indications of it in her caountenance.'

Clearly, this raconteur was a conscious humorist, with an audience. Dry, but not so dry that almost any listener might not get a bit of refreshment from it. There must have been a twinkle or a twitch that betrayed him.

The same may generally be said, I think, of other typically American humor of the dry variety. One may be sure Lincoln indulged in an inward chuckle that showed in tone or eye if not in actual laughter. When Mark Twain said, on receiving an honorary degree, that he never doctored any literature, he may have enjoyed his little joke, but he certainly counted on his audience's enjoying it too. And when Whistler retorted in print to one of his critics, 'Who ever supposed you were a real person?' — he must have hoped that the critic would wince *just because* others would see the joke. Of your dyed-in-the-wool Cape humorist, on the contrary, it can be said that he gets rather more pleasure if you don't see the joke. He is not quite at home with a responsive audience.

Now I don't mean to be doctrinaire. There are no exact boundaries to humor, and the genuine Cape Cod variety appears in somewhat diluted form in other parts of New England. But it rarely goes west of the Berkshires. Once in the Hudson valley, during an exceptionally dry, hot spell in June, I passed some workmen toiling near a dazzling concrete walk. 'Guess we'll be cutting ice on that sidewalk to-day,' one of them said to me with a serious drawl. From long acquaintance with more eastern folk, I responded, quite as seriously as he, 'Ought to get quite a crop.' Perhaps they do not speak of an ice *crop* along the Hudson, but from the contemptuous glance the man gave me, I feel sure he was disappointed with my sense of humor. He had made a joke and, instead of laughing, I had taken him seriously!

One of the best examples of what I have designated as Cape Cod humor, but in this case made outside the sacred precincts, is the reply ascribed to Mr. Coolidge, when, as Vice-President, he was rallied at a dinner-party by a lady who assured him that she had a bet she could make him converse.

'Well, ma'am,' he is reported to have said, 'you've lost your bet.'

But, though Cape Cod humor takes its merit

from its complete lack of what is humorous elsewhere, a visitor to southeastern Massachusetts
makes a great mistake if he supposes that these
Cape folk don't mean to be funny. Sometimes he
laughs at them, if the thrust is not too personal, as
he laughs at unintentional Scotch humor. But he
is grossly in error. When your genuine clam-digger
on the Cape delivers himself of preposterous in-
congruities with a straight face, you may not see
the joke, but it is there, even if you don't see it —
especially if you don't see it. From other New
England humor it may differ in degree rather than
in kind, but it alone is the simon-pure, sand-dry,
salt-cured article.

The most perfect instance I know is the reply
of a Buzzards' Bay native to President Cleveland.
Cleveland had missed his way after a long day's
fishing. It was pouring rain; he was afoot. When
he knocked at the door of a lonely farmhouse, a
voice from a second-floor window asked him what
he wanted.

'I want to stay here to-night,' called the
President.

'Well,' replied the voice, 'stay there.'

THE BEAN TEST

ONCE a year I become an earnest bean-picker. Along about the hottest day in July, the beans decide that they 'want' to be picked. At least, so the lady who is going to cold-pack them says. She doesn't work in a refrigerator, in spite of the name she gives her mysteries, but in a kitchen, and, as I said, she chooses the hottest day in the year; so I can hardly complain if she wishes me to enjoy a little sympathetic sizzling in the bean-patch. Anyhow, she herself is above picking beans. She's a skilled craftsman, an artist. She has attained the sublimation wherein, after adding the heat of a kitchen stove to July at its darnedest, she is able, with an esoteric gleam, to believe that what she is doing is really the *cold*-pack method.

Now bean-picking is one of the lowest forms of human activity. The lowest is bean-eating. Such kindred activities as blueberry-picking may be rated lower, too, I suppose, because there is always the lure of a rake-off for the furtive picker. But what are you to do with filched beans? Also, God did not ordain that blueberries might not be gathered in the cool dawn. No, there are specious attractions to berry-picking which render it unfit, as a test, to compete with bean-picking.

Not that I would exalt the humble bean-picker. I have just admitted that he is measurably lower than the angels in the kitchen. Though he requires a certain amount of fortitude, he doesn't require much strength or skill. But he has his points. Don't mistake me, reader. I am not referring to the gathering of a mess for supper — a mere couple of quarts — with the succulent reward of your virtue only a few hours distant. I mean picking for the red-hot cold-pack process — picking bushels, wheelbarrows. Well, that kind of bean-picking has its points.

I have mentioned the kind of day the canning expert selects. I have alluded to the time of day God has assigned to the bean-picker. 'Daylight Saving' is of no avail; at ten o'clock 'Standard' he begins and not a minute before unless he is willing to risk the 'rust,' a plague in which God and the Devil seem to work in collusion. Nimble little fingers that might share the work seem to be needed in the kitchen. He is left alone with the beans and the sun. Perhaps it is just as well, though; for I find that on those rare occasions when I have coadjutors, I glean basketfuls from rows that are supposed to have been covered. Not that I pretend to be a really great bean-picker; but I think, in all modesty, that I may be said to have a nose for beans.

Along with such a nose your perfect bean-gatherer should possess what the athletic people call 'a great pair of hands.' In fact, the whole man, it may be said, is called into play. To squat for hours and yet to squat with such subtle variations that the knees do not stick fast is in itself no mean feat — it requires a great pair of knees. And then the eyes! As in other phases of life, one must look before and after. It is astonishing how different a bean looks from behind. Even the brain is not wholly idle, for there must be instantaneous selection, without massaging each pod, of those beans which really 'want' to be picked. The sympathetic reader may readily conceive how painful it is to an accomplished bean-picker to see misfits pulling the bushes to pieces and dropping the pods one by one into the basket. Indeed, the final accomplishment of the master-picker is to pick handfuls with a rhythmic, sweeping gesture — not violent, so that the bushes are torn asunder, but without making deposits in the basket till the hand is quite full. This process of course requires the picker to open the hand before each new pod is added and yet to close it before any of the old pods slip out. My proficiency in this respect, if I may call it such, I attribute to nothing so much as to a youth assiduously spent in playing jack-stones.

It should be clear from the foregoing, without

laboring the point, that there are great varieties and degrees among bean-pickers. I have often wondered, in fact, whether the expression, 'Shucks! He ain't worth beans!' might not originally have applied to a man's capacity as a picker. I shall be told, I fear, that the expression stood for capital, that any one 'not worth beans' was poor indeed. But I like to believe that it stood for capacity. How many men accounted competent and successful, could we take them out a-picking, might prove to be actually *not worth beans!*

In fact, I have long fancied that bean-picking might be used as a universal test of low-grade capacity. In the absence of Exacticus I hesitate to put the idea forward seriously, but it *would be* a splendidly accurate and simple form of measurement. Instead of complicated intelligence tests, with only a harvest of papers at the end of the day, you would get a crop of beans garnered while the simple process was searching out and setting in order all sorts of applicants for academic or industrial promotion. It is true, of course, that the method might be found difficult in northern climates during winter, yet no doubt a synthetic bean could be devised.

But the great advantage, in addition to the simplicity and economic saving, would lie in the fact that the test would really find out what we want to know. It does not seem to occur to the contrivers of intelligence tests that any high-grade moron is likely to be required to do things with his hands quite as much as with his head. Of what avail that he can tell which word is correct in a given puzzle-sentence or that he can under favorable conditions reproduce a series of figures? Here he is raw from school applying for a job at factory, office, or farm. Of course he doesn't know much; for a while he will have to do chores. It would be a comfort to dispense with the gratuitous misinformation with which his application is usually accompanied and to know simply whether he has the elementary capacity to pick beans — to know, in addition to the fact that his mind is at least twelve years old, that he has perseverance and 'a great pair of hands.'

Consider, too, how the bean-test would simplify the problem of immigration. The embarrassment of Gertrude Ederle at Dover (and also of the official, let us hope) was the result of red tape. Yet even a customs official could see at a glance that it would be an effrontery to question *her* capacity — like the lady in 'Hyperion,' 'she could have ta'en Achilles by the hair and bent his neck.' Or the Countess Cathcart embarrassment on our side. Secretary Kellogg need only have asked, 'Can she pick beans?' Over the wire would probably have come the reply, 'She *won't*' — *voilà*, the problem solved!

If I were Uncle Sam, I should want to know, of peasants coming from Europe, not whether they could read and write, but whether they could pick beans.

KIPLING, PIONEER

'THE Vineyard' has brought Kipling into notice again. Diners-out and that large section of the populace who seek excitement as letter-writers to the papers are violent about the poem. But they aren't discussing it as poetry; in fact, most of them don't know the poetry of Kipling.

Of course it is not astonishing for diners-out and letter-writers at large to be ignorant of most poetry. But Kipling! Why, thirty years ago everybody was reading him, and every other body had poem after poem by heart. Yet, though the publishers still sell sets of Kipling, who reads him? Ask almost any one under forty; that is, any one who was seventeen or less in 1903, when 'The Five Nations' appeared. One might as well talk Ostrogothic as quote him to the rising generation.

All this oblivion is easy enough to account for, I suppose. Publishers will tell you that most readers 'pluck the near and the green.' Now Kipling is no longer near and green; wherefore we read his imitators — until the next publishing turnover, when we shall read the imitators of his imitators. The final step, when copyrights run out, will be to put him into schoolbooks, and then everybody will be brought up on him. The real measure of a writer, evidently, is not whether he succeeds in the next generation (that would be preposterous if flivverous publishers are to startle and waylay us with novelties), but whether he gets into the schoolbooks in the third generation.

Of course Kipling will come back. Eventually — why not now! For, to a pedestrian way of seeing things, he is the real pioneer of modern poetry.

Not so much a pioneer in prose, he nevertheless caught the short story while it was still young and plastic and, after Stevenson was dead, surpassed all his contemporaries. And though he has never been much of a hand at creating great characters (barring Mowgli, Mulvaney, and perhaps Kim), he has been a master at striking off vivid types, such as Ortheris, Learoyd, and Anglo-Indian gentry at play; while he has left the writers of animal stories, as Sir Anthony Gloster did the shipowners, 'sweating and stealing a year and a half behind.' *Uncle Remus* is the only thing since the Middle Ages that can hold a candle to Kipling in the 'beast-tale' line. In fact, I'm not sure that Akela and Rikki-tikki-tavi oughtn't to be listed with his great characters.

The things that mark Kipling's prose, moreover, mark his poetry. His keen sense for local color, his eye for detail, his grasp of a situation and the humor and pathos of it — these are obvious virtues which set him off from the run of literature, from the craven literature which, quartered, is ever one part wisdom and three parts imitation.

But his poetry is more than fresh and vigorous. It reveals a new art and a new life. To speak of Kipling as new seems a little odd, no doubt, with so many 'new' fads and fancies since the day of his popularity. But it is just because most of these new movements, where they have had any value, find their roots in him that it seems, to a pedestrian mind, really odd to treat him as old-fashioned.

Looking out from a hilltop where the gyrating flivvers are left behind, one observes that with the passing of Tennyson the old order fell into corruption. Swinburne was growing old, and anyhow he was something like the Irish sailor taking soundings who made a harmonious, unintelligible noise and who, when asked to repeat what he said, replied, 'Well, I don't exactly know the worruds, but I've got the chune all right.' Minor voices, feebly imitating Tennyson, mouthing 'cosmic phrases,' were in the air. Poetry was bankrupt.

New voices, at first scarcely audible, gradually reached the public ear. By 1910 the NEW POETRY (small caps) was a fact; by 1917 Amy Lowell reset it in large caps — NEW POETRY.

Now what are some of the characteristics of this New Poetry? At least, what durable qualities has it which it did not inherit from the Victorians? A new realism, for one thing — a sense of fact; an inclination to call a spade a spade, if not, as some one has said, a 'damned shovel.' Kipling all over. A new and stirring type of narrative — in Masefield's hands probably the best since Chaucer, certainly the best since Scott and Byron. But Kipling broke the ground for Masefield, as indeed for Noyes; and he ploughed and harrowed and sowed for Service.

Among all the gestures of the Imagist School none was so real as their ridicule of vague, 'cosmic phrases' and their insistence on images that should be 'hard and clear.' But who, a generation before the Imagists, broke through the fogs of contemporary poetry with language as 'hard and clear' as the sun-bright images of the African veld? This sense for the concrete, for the telling phrase that 'tells' just because it makes you see and hear, is the very center of Kipling's art. True, he loves to mouth a fine phrase, even in his best verse, and he gets up a kind of tinsel romance by frequent mention of strange Oriental places (did not Coleridge conjure with 'Xanadu' and Keats with 'Samarcand'?); but in the modern vogue for 'the exact word' and the striking image he surpasses, as he precedes, them all. A good instance is in 'The Bell Buoy':

> 'The beach-pools cake and skim,
> The bursting spray-heads freeze,

I gather on crown and rim
    The gray, grained ice of the seas.'

or 'the wind is as thin as a whip-lash,' or

'Ebb of Yokohama Bay
    Swigs chattering through the buoys.'

Try it and see. You can get the swing of Kipling's
verse, you can look up and introduce the strange
Oriental places, you can mouth a magnificent re-
frain; you can write a pretty good *imitation*, but
your despair will be the phrase that bites in.

When it comes to verse-form, Kipling of course
has had nothing to do with the modern attempt to
omit the form, sometimes even the verse. (This
must be what is meant by Symbolism — lacking
both verse and form, you just guess.) But if freedom *within the limits of metre* be considered, here
also he has been a pioneer. Few have shown more
clearly what can be done, in a simple measure, by
shift of stress and quantity, as in

'You'll hear the long-drawn thunder'

or

'It's up and over the tongue of Jagai'

or

'Their hoofs drum up the dawn.'

Further, he has been the first since the Anglo-
Saxons, so far as I know, to use successfully a four-

stress line with an indeterminate number of minor syllables.

'Thús saith the Lórd in the váult above the Chérubim'

or

'There's a whísper down the fiéld where the yeár has shot her yíeld.'

These are not dactyls and trochees; it is an idle and fruitless practice to count the syllables on your fingers and toes.

Somewhere Stevenson speaks contemptuously of poets 'puling in little atheistical poetry books.' As one sees them pule and hears them babble vainly of their New Poetry and then considers what of the new has quality enough to grow old, he discerns that the genuine New Poet of our age, the worthy pioneer, is the man the public treats as old-fashioned. Kipling probably did not have himself in mind when he wrote 'The Explorer'; but if he did, he might with justice cry, 'O my prophetic soul!' —

'They'll go back and do the talking. *They'll* be called the pioneers.'

PROTESTANTISM — DEAD OR ASLEEP?

CANON HANNAY, in the April 'Forum,' presents a vivid picture of the breakdown of English Protestantism, at least in the Anglican Church. He assumes the rôle of reporter, moreover; not of propagandist. He observes recent Church history and writes down the facts and the explanation of the facts as he sees them. He's 'not argufyin',' he's just a-tellin' us.'

That's all to the good. Mr. Chesterton, 'argufyin',' had almost persuaded us to thank God we were Protestants. Now Canon Hannay, if his picture is a true one, if this be Protestantism, or even one important phase of it, fairly persuades us to thank God for its demise. The only trouble is, the corpse isn't Protestantism. It is a large part of external Protestantism, to be sure; and many Protestants themselves mistake it for the real thing — just as a good many Americans mistake a complexity of laws plus a total disregard of laws for Democracy.

Not that I question Canon Hannay's statement of fact, nor yet his inferences from the facts he selects. My contention is merely that he omits the really important facts. He appears to assume that the choice must be between old priest and new evangelist, precisely as a good many people of Milton's day supposed it must be between 'old priest' and 'New Presbyter'; but it is difficult to see just where Dean Inge, or any genuine Protestant, fits into that picture.

The breakdown pictured by Canon Hannay has come, he says, in three steps: first, a theological débâcle; then, a ritualistic; finally, a devotional. Well, you don't have to go to England to find plenty of evidence for his statement. Witness the frantic propaganda among the churches; there is evidently so little virtue in make-believe Protestantism that its adherents must 'sell' it with advertising campaigns. Or observe the wholly un-Protestant attempts of various sects to establish temporal power, either as sects or through political organizations devilishly organized in the name of God. The violent intolerance prevalent is another confession of failure; desperate sects, losing ground, are making laws and fighting to preserve their prejudices precisely as Rome did before them in the fifteenth century. Then there are the worldlings, often Protestants in their own esteem. Indeed, little reveals the breakdown of fustian Protestantism more than the following advertisement of a well-known railroad:

This is the Lenten Season at Atlantic City and Asbury Park. . . . The recreations and entertainments are delightfully diverting. . . . Fashion in her latest modes holds court with her most brilliant and loyal devotees.

So this is Lent! These railroad people are not advertising for fun; they know whom they are addressing — new-rich Jews, pagans, and that great body we loosely and erroneously term Protestants.

The failure of so-called Protestantism is obvious enough. Analyzed, it no doubt amounts, among the more serious, to theological, ritualistic, and devotional breakdown, all in the proper order, just as Canon Hannay points out. That would account for a large defection. But this defection, large as it may be in numbers, doesn't touch the heart and the only true hope of Protestantism. If it clears the ground by taking the defectives to Rome or Atlantic City — so much the better for Protestantism.

Protestantism, if it has meant anything worth living and dying for during four centuries, has meant a state of mind which refuses temporal authority in spiritual matters. It is true that historical Protestantism has concerned itself greatly with ritual, doctrine, and secular power, with what L. P. Jacks calls 'carnal logic,' and with what Jesus called 'the things of Cæsar.' Protestant sects have denied their life-principle over and over again by doing the very things they essentially protest against. They have done their best to destroy one another with one hand while they were strangling themselves with the other. But surely their perversions have not kept them going. Rather, Protestants have kept going in spite of their carnal logic (and latterly in spite of what among the Anglicans may be called a sort of vegetarian logic); they have endured because the best of them were not really interested in doctrine or ritual or temporal power, but in what John Milton called 'liberty of conscience.' They have appeared to protest against transubstantiation, but at bottom they have been protesting against autocracy. To them *any* 'forcers of conscience' (Papist, Anglican, Calvinist, Wesleyan) are fundamentally tyrannical.

Luther, for instance, was a genuine Protestant when he stood up on the Scala Sancta and protested in favor of a free conscience. He was merely an ingenious heretic when he quibbled about the sacrament. Wiclif, similarly, played both rôles. At a time when doctrine seemed to matter tremendously it was difficult to keep clear of theological controversy. It was just as difficult, a short time after, for the followers of Knox to avoid organizing for temporal power. Among the founders of Protestant sects, George Fox was perhaps the first Englishman to refuse both fashions —that of organizing a water-tight doctrine and that of organizing for temporal power. Even the Wesleyans, with the examples of Romanist and Puritan before them, have gone more or less the same road, till now, in the twentieth century, they are doing crudely what the Catholics have for centuries done well. The Methodist Church, Bishop Hughes said the other day in Philadelphia, 'God saw fit to create in appropriate time in order that it might be ready when this Country was born. . . . We have the spiritual responsibility for the United States of America.' Surely no one discerns any vestiges of real Protestantism in *that!*

Genuine spiritual heirs of Luther the Protestant, as distinguished from Luther the Theologian, have frequently been identified with no church. Milton, not Hooker, for example; Coleridge, not Wilberforce; Emerson and Carlyle, not Pusey. These men have not been contentious over creeds and rituals; they have not turned to secular authority for religion; they have not put faith in a stampeded and short-lived ecstasy miscalled devotion. They have not been religious in any of the ways Canon Hannay appears to think necessary, yet they have been the great Protestants, its driving force, the faithful guardians of the lamp of religious liberty. For they have kept always before them the essential principle — freedom of conscience. To them, as Carlyle puts it, make-believe sect-religion is futile and 'may go and dwell among the Brahmins, Antinomians, Spinning Dervishes, or where it will; with me it shall have no harbor.' Or as

Emerson: 'We are now men . . . not minors and
invalids in a protected corner. . . . advancing on
Chaos and the Dark.'

The same alignment, moreover, still continues.
On the side of Luther the Protestant, men like
L. P. Jacks, Dean Inge, Rufus Jones, Dr. Fosdick;
on the side of Luther the theologian — well, in
Milton's phrase, those 'timorous and flocking
birds' who 'in their envious gabble would prognos-
ticate a year of sects and schisms.'

It is easy to see, of course, that this sort of
Protestantism, perhaps the only Protestantism
worth having, may not number many conven-
tional Christians. Self-reliance easily turns to arrogance, and arrogance breeds new tyrannies. Its
principle, moreover, is by nature centrifugal; it is
in its healthiest state when it is breeding heretics.
It is more likely to produce a Voltaire than an
Archbishop Laud. Further, it must always lack
the popular appeal of worldly organizations, for its
only possible bond is one of spiritual sympathy.
In considering the demise of Protestantism, however, this central heart of it cannot be blithely
ignored. It is, in fact, the only thing about Protestantism that is really Protestant. To leave it
out is to omit the leaven, to rest content with a
sour and sodden loaf.

The defection of a large number of Anglicans
to Romanism, in other words, is not significant

because it satisfies some doctrinal, ritualistic, or emotional-devotional urge. A Pedestrian mind finds it difficult to see why two sacraments are better than seven or why the ritualist should not have 'Reservation' and 'Benediction' to any extent he wishes. As George Fox said to William Penn, 'Wear thy sword as long as thou *canst.*' The really significant question is whether liberalism in religion is dying. Are these Anglicans merely adopting Roman forms of worship or are they accepting the Papacy? That's one phase of the important question. The other is: How many, in proportion to those turning Romewards, are turning in the opposite direction? — not always, by any means, into this or that sect, but perhaps into the growing body of earnest people who, like the Chinaman, want to see Christianity tried.

This question is all the more significant because it coincides roughly with the political issue between liberalism and autocracy. If the western world really turns Fascist or Bolshevist, as it somewhat threatens to do, if all kinds of liberalism are as undesirable as the discredited liberalism of the nineteenth century, then freedom of conscience might as well give up too.

SHIBBOLETH

SOME years ago the pangs of hunger led my vagabond feet to a small restaurant in Richmond, Vermont — an eating-house not greatly celebrated for its food, perhaps, but forever memorable to me on account of a notice writ large on the wall. Looking up between forkfuls of pie, I found myself solicited by a sign to this effect:

SMOKE UP. NUFF SAID

What a hospitable place, I thought, to invite the weary traveler to smoke in tranquillity, perhaps even to indulge in meditation, while he masters the beans and pie peculiar to this sturdy neighborhood. With twenty miles of open road and windy weald behind me, and with my old dudeen strangely sweet and drawing like the funnel of a tramp in the Trades, I was just sinking gently into the contentment which transcends mere cogitation when the rude voice of the proprietor called out, 'Hey, you can't smoke here.' I made a luxurious gesture toward the sign. 'Oh,' he said with a scornful laugh; 'it don't mean *that way*.'

Since that rude awakening, it has been frequently borne in upon me that people have a singularly

persistent way of misinterpreting signs and wonders. Not less singular, perhaps, is the disposition
to cling to their misinterpretation. Usually, to
be sure, they cling with a molluscular inertia, because it is the easiest thing to do, but some of them
cling desperately, as a drowning man with no
alternative, while not a few get themselves into
a sort of militancy through their very act of clinging. This characteristic is particularly prevalent
when they take hold of a big word with little
meaning, like 'Democracy,' or of a little word
with big meaning, like 'Truth,' or when they
subscribe to saws and proverbs that everybody has
believed time out of mind. It must have been a
dyspeptic old crone who invented the cheerful lie
that you can't have your cake and eat it too. Any
small boy knows better, and he is blithely indifferent to the old crone's foot-note that she didn't
mean it 'that way.' There's only one way to
have cake worth having.

Similarly, we are told, with solemnity akin to
piety, that 'Speech is silver, but silence is golden'
— as if silence, in comparison to speech that is
really silver (not just German silver or sounding
brass), had any virtue at all except in so far as it
punctuates speech. 'Still waters run deep' is another notion to which vain repetition has committed mankind. Many a silent blockhead, entrenched behind this miserable formula, has laid

the flattering unction of depth to his soul. And even in this day of domestic infelicity, people have the effrontery to tell you that too many cooks spoil the broth. Tandem, perhaps they do. I have known a succession of cooks to spoil the broth, but in this century I find it hard to visualize a team of cooks. I should like to give them a chance.

Some literal heckler in the audience is due, about now, to remind me that people don't mean these sayings 'that way.' Of course they don't. These random instances will have served my purpose if they raise the suspicion that they mean about as much one way as the other.

Many centuries ago, we are told, the men of Gilead found that the Ephraimites could not say the word 'shibboleth'; so it was selected as a test word. If, after the rout at the passages of Jordan, a captured straggler failed to pass the test, he was indisputably an Ephraimite and was put to the sword. But if he could pronounce the magic word, he was at once accepted into the bosom of the family. It didn't matter whether he meant 'ear of corn' or 'Jordan' when he said it; the great thing was to be able to say it with accuracy and dispatch. Is it base cynicism to suppose that our army of word-warriors has fixed on a similar test? If the poor straggler can say the right words, he runs a fair chance of getting past the sentries. But now and then a sentry with more honesty than discretion has the temerity to ask, 'Just what does "shibboleth" mean?'

The other day I met such a sentry — a lady of eighty with a confirmed inclination to prefer Emerson to Freud. I had just read her an ingenious article in which the terms 'psychology' and 'civilization' were freely used. For myself, I was ready to spend half an hour discussing the value of the article, determining, so to speak, whether the author could not only *say* 'shibboleth,' but could also *interpret* it. But the old lady gave him less than half a minute. 'Oh,' she cried, 'all this talk about psychology and civilization — and *no enlightenment!*'

Turning to the newspaper, my eye caught sight of the following morsel (choice, I carelessly supposed), and I read it to her: 'Unfortunately the amplifier cannot enlarge the thought.' But true to form, she replied quickly: '*Fortunately* the amplifier cannot enlarge the thought!'

It is no cynicism at all, I fear, but the simple fact, that most of us indulge in a romantic worship of 'shibboleth,' of any saying which means little to us but which serves as a password with the sentries. 'The law is the law' is one of the phrases behind which we love to conceal 'scant tracks of thought.' Of course Law, as an abstract principle or as the concrete statement of a universally accepted principle, is just as different from a collection of statutes as Truth is from a collection of facts. A moment's reflection tells us that *the* law, the statute, may be a practical expression of custom or the fanatical expression of an organized minority; a necessity, a convenience, a nuisance; — just as various, in fact, as furniture or church doctrine, or any other man-made thing. It would be quite as sensible to entrench ourselves, in defense of the study of Latin or of the consumption of jam, behind such phrases as 'Latin is Latin' or 'Jam is jam.' So it is — no question!

But the magical power of the word 'Law' is no new thing. When it is worked into such a phrase as 'Public Liberty under Law,' it can tease us out of thought as doth Eternity. In some sort of way we have believed in the mysterious virtue of the *word* (not merely in the value of law, a very different thing) since the dawn of our history. Did not William of Normandy know the shibboleth? We imagine perhaps that he made his conquest at Senlac, Chester, and Ely; but *he* knew perfectly well that his chief victory lay in his promise to respect 'Edward's Law.' He broke his promise when he found it convenient to do so; for the phrase, not the meaning of it, was what counted.

Now our equivalent for 'Edward's Law' is 'Public Liberty under Law,' and any one who contemplates conquering America had better practice the phrase. On a recent visit to Boston, having

spare time at my disposal, I took occasion to re-
visit some of the historic monuments. Stopping
before the Old South Church, I read an inscription
which announced that

HERE THE MEN OF BOSTON PROVED THEM-
SELVES BRAVE INDEPENDENT FREEMEN
WORTHY TO WIN AND TRANSMIT PUBLIC
LIBERTY UNDER LAW

I read it again; then I said (I supposed, to myself),
'Just what *is* "public liberty"?' But I must have
thought out loud, for a man near me remarked,
'That's just what I was going to ask *you*.'

For the present, though, it seems to be enough
to know what the inscription says; to be able, as it
were, to pronounce 'shibboleth.' It is an imperti-
nent assumption of private liberty to wonder what
it means. But I should like to know what my old
lady would say if she did Boston the honor to walk
down Washington Street and read the inscription.

THE CHAMBER OF HORRORS

ALL right. We'll put you in the Chamber of Horrors.

That from a Philadelphia hostess, to whom I had been so far discourteous as to object that her guest room at the front of the house was no place for a decent body to sleep. The roar of traffic all night long gave one a lively sense of having couched inadvertently at the intersection of Forty-Second Street and Lexington Avenue, New York.

The Chamber of Horrors is at the back of an old fore-and-aft house one room wide and half a block long. The room is fairly high up (I know from looking out the window), but to get to it you go down as well as up, down and up, till you are not quite sure of your elevation. When I leave the Chamber in quest of breakfast, I am never certain whether I shall find myself in the attic or the cellar till the smell of inhabited regions and the unfriendly roar of traffic give me at last a strong sense of direction.

The room was fairly large once, but a bathroom has been nibbled out of one corner, and out of the other a huge closet of matched boards painted white. I call it a closet only out of courtesy, for, though commodious, it is quite full of large boxes,

142

a pair of riding-boots, elderly valises, a set of old chest-pulls, and a great many coat-hangers with no visible space for coats. Clearly it is not intended for guests. It might be a henhouse so far as outward appearance goes and may properly be designated as Horror No. 1.

Reassured on my first visit by the bed (Blessing No. 1), I looked about me. My eye caught next a fine old mahogany bureau, a piece provocative of theft (Blessing No. 2). From it I turned to Horror No. 2, a yellow chest of drawers in the authentic church-pew pattern of 1875, drawers all full of boxes and things somebody couldn't bear to throw away. Opposite it, and an unhappy foil to the henhouse, stands a gigantic wardrobe of golden oak, period of 1890. This piece is definitely ugly and is so large that it may reasonably pass as two Horrors, Nos. 3 and 4. The first time I saw it, though, my heart leapt up with high hope that here at least a coat or two could be hung. Alas, no; plenty of coat-hangers, but, like the henhouse, chock-a-block with boxes and bundles. I have since learned to hang my coat on one of the dining-room chairs, which help, with a marble-top table, to fill up the remaining space. No harm in that, either, for the floor is painted the color of tomato soup and wants hiding. To this end four small and shabby but quite genuine Oriental rugs do worthy service.

From the foregoing sketch the reader will discern that it is a most attractive room. In fact, I have come to love it, to love even the glimpses of tomato soup and the effrontery of the glaring white henhouse. I still hate the wardrobe, but I have given up kicking it and in course of time I think I may develop a sort of affection for it, even for it.

Challenged to explain why I love this musty old room, I think I should find the reason in its dogged air of permanence. Here things have come to stay — things which don't fit in elsewhere, which often enough are fairly hideous, but which find a place in the expansive heart of a lumber-room. There are more superficial reasons, of course. The room is quiet beyond belief. Also it is a complete repudiation of Babbitt and all his works. It indulges your vanity, too: sitting at the marble-top table, you have an irresistible feeling that you must look like Charles Sumner about to sign something important. But the real secret, I am sure, lies in the air of permanence. Life in this room is not just a debilitating succession of ephemera. It has roots and gradual growth, continuity. Yet it is haphazard and kaleidoscopic, too, as it ought to be; not precise and ordered, like a machine. Man in his diviner moments can make beautiful rooms; in his more devilish, he can make ugly rooms: he is pretty good at heaven or hell.

But he couldn't make this room, not if he called in all the upstanding Rotarians and recumbent æsthetes in Christendom. It has made itself — full of horrors, full of blessings, dead yet alive, tawdry yet magnificent.

The pictures tell the same story. In the first place, there are too many of them. Nature always overproduces. Subtract wall space necessary for a door, two windows, a bureau, a henhouse, and the golden oak wardrobe (which I am sorry to mention again) and then make room, if you can, for eighteen pictures. But there they are; some of them dreadful (one at least I shall simply forbear to name), some of them good, two of them rare. As samples take a nondescript photograph of the Kremlin and square, Moscow; a large photograph of Rossetti's lady combing her hair (this colored and beautifully framed); three German pictures of the rural-domestic school — 'Was hat die Mutter mitgebracht?' 'Blindekuhspiel,' and 'Verunglückte Schlittenfahrt.' (These three suggest that there ought to be a couple of samplers and antimacassars, but after all life is at best fragmentary.) Then there is a small copy of a Dürer woodcut, an atrocious engraving of a landscape in a heavy Victorian frame (florid-horrid style), and two etchings of trees by Martine — rather nice when, as, and if you get past the frames. Also (not least!) a Meissonier etching of a soldier

145

riding in the wind and an original by Hokusai —
a delightful little picture of two ladies in a snow-
storm. (Memo. would go handily in one of the
drawers when you steal the bureau.)

These pictures, like the furniture, fairly talk to
you of the life lived in this old house during a half-
century. Downstairs there are improvements,
concealments, but here the secret is plain. And if
I seem to overstep the bounds of courtesy in
making public the mysteries of my hosts, I am
sure they are secrets to be proud of. We open the
family closet and reveal, not a skeleton at all, but
the record of a rich and varied past. The owners
call it the Chamber of Horrors. Perverse generation! If they only knew, it is the Chamber of
Blessings!

Consider the books. There is no wall space for
a real bookcase (that will be clear, even if I don't
mention the golden oak wardrobe again), but the
henhouse is only six feet high, and along the front
edge of its roof stands a goodly row of books.
They ought all to be listed, every one of the
hundred and five volumes, to give a true impression, but I shall have to content myself with types
and be as fair as I can.

  1. 'The Digressions of V,' by Elihu Vedder.
       (Several other oldish art books of which this is
       a fair specimen.)
  2. Six volumes by Howard Pyle.

146

3. Eleven volumes of Dickens, including 'Dombey,' 'Bleak House,' and 'Christmas Stories.'

 (This alone puts the shelf in the running with Dr. Eliot's.)

4. 'A Family Flight over Egypt and Syria,' by *Rev.* Edward E. Hale and *Miss* Susan Hale.

 (Italics mine, thinking how nowadays people like William Lawrence leave the labels off.)

5. 'Mammy Tittleback,' by 'H.H.'

6. 'The Little Duke,' by Charlotte Yonge.

7. 'Pennsylvania Dutch,' by 'G.'

 (At first I thought the initial might stand for 'God,' both from the author's seriousness and from the fact that the first chapter originally appeared in the 'Atlantic Monthly,' but coming later upon several references to 'Mrs. G.,' I discarded the conjecture as improbable.)

8. 'Gösta Berling,' by Selma Lagerlöf.

9. 'The Fairy Land of Science,' by Arabella Buckley, 1883.

 (Contains a frontispiece of a 'glacier carrying down stones' and spreading them with as great precision as the machines at Niagara distribute shredded wheat.)

10. 'The Mason Bees,' by Fabre.

11. 'The Country of the Pointed Firs,' by Sarah Orne Jewett.

12. 'The Life of Alice Freeman Palmer,' by G. H. Palmer.

13. 'The Joyous Adventures of Aristide Pujol,' by W. J. Locke.

14. 'Holy Bible,' Revised Version.

 (Look before and after — O democracy of letters!)

15. 'Tono-Bungay,' by H. G. Wells.

Multiply by seven and you have a rare book-shelf — a revelation, if I may steal and pervert Miss Repplier's phrase, of the really-truly 'happy half-century.' Just to look at the backs of these books is an experience. To spend a week-end with them is to realize 'infinite riches in a little room.'

THOSE VICTORIANS

YOUNG people are strongly *either — or* people. And since this is decidedly a period when youth is in the saddle (bit in the horse's teeth, too), the articulate world appears to be given violently to alternatives. So they are quarreling again about the Victorians. Oddly enough, though, they appear to agree on their definition of the word.

That must have been a stuffy time (if you are a liberated soul) — a time when people were eminently respectable, when children were dutiful and suppressed, when ladies were distinctly different from mere women. How much better our frank modern days, when we open the windows wide to the strong winds of truth. Or (if you are a reactionary) those were 'the good old times,' when, thank God, people *were* respectable and children *were* dutiful. Stuffy perhaps, but far better than our modern breezy days, when the wind bloweth whither it listeth! At least they knew enough to shut the windows during a storm.

It is not astonishing, of course, that one group blasphemes and the other worships this image of Victorianism they have set up. The really astonishing thing is that they should both consider the image authentic. The defenders are fighting a losing battle when they weakly accept the false picture which the contemners have drawn. For the result is, since the emancipated brethren think Victorians were prigs and hypocrites, that the conservatives, in sweet antiphony, are busy singing the virtues of the defects.

Yet there are still a good many living who grew up before the century turned, who can recall something better than Victorianism on its last legs. Their childhood antedates the common use of telephone and automobile, even of trolley-car. They can remember the leisurely times when the residential districts of Boston, Philadelphia, and Baltimore, even of New York, bore something of the small town neighborliness that still appears in the stories of Mr. Booth Tarkington. Those with a more rural background recall the days that antedated 'tourists,' renovated inns, oiled roads, hot-dog dug-outs, movies, noise, speed — 'the days of real sport,' when 'two fingers' meant the swimming-hole to the younger generation and a drink of unadulterated liquor to the full-blown male.

Now these are not conspicuous virtues in themselves. Neither, on the other hand, is there *per se* any virtue in 'running to and fro upon the earth like frightened sheep.' To extol or condemn merely the outward manifestations gets us off the track. They are the regular red herrings used by the devil to keep disputants busy. What matters is the life back of those manifestations — back of the leisure and neighborliness and real sport, back of the modern manifestation of speed and noise.

We might as well admit, in preface, a good measure of the smugness and hypocrisy which the contemners put into the picture. Youth, particularly male youth, is better off in many ways than it was in Victorian days. The middle-aged male, too, is a simpler, more genuine human being — less of a shirt front. Even woman, whose nature is so much more fundamental than her new freedom, retains her charm in spite of herself. As for groups of people — classes, nations — 'the world do move,' if slowly, and better conditions are discernible in all sorts of ways. It is a sorry sentimentalist who regrets the passing of the 'gentleman' and of underfed, underpaid labor; and it is a sorrier cynic who believes that we have made no progress whatever towards peace among nations. It is true that 'the electric light will not dispel the darkness of the mind,' but neither will a tallow dip or the 'flaring gas-lights' of a Victorian London.

Grant all that. There was a virtue, nevertheless, which lay back of the small town neighborliness and 'the days of real sport.' It wasn't peculiar to Victorian times, but it ceased rather abruptly with the development of the telephone and the automobile. It was the condition imposed by the

inability to communicate. Ever since the beginning
of things man has been seeking to communicate
with his fellows; and it seems a perverse notion to
view his recent success as a disaster. Well, of
course it isn't, in many senses. Better understanding of one another, increased knowledge of
the world, speedy relief of distress — one can
think of many ways in which modern means of
communication spell progress. But there is one
thing which they have shut out — the necessity
of getting along with your neighbors and with
yourself — and so far they have provided no
substitute. It begins to emerge that mere *ability*
to communicate is in itself no better than mere
inability to communicate. The latter may produce
a mental stagnancy; the former, a mental whirl-
pool.

Now the much maligned Victorian days, to my
ways of thinking, provided just about the right
amount of communication. You were not in the
desperate state of the rustic who answered, when
asked how he spent his winter evenings, 'Well,
sometimes I set an' think, an' sometimes I just
set.' Nor were you in the desperate state of him
who blurts, 'Sorry — call me again in half an
hour,' or who rushes from the table to the telephone as one seasick to the rail. There were long
periods when you were thrown back on yourself,
to devise what entertainment you could, when

the family was thrown back on itself, or on its immediate neighbors, when you could not at a moment's notice reorganize life, for golf or bridge or a movie party — anything to escape the tedium of yourself and your intolerable family!

Thence proceeded some of the most durable satisfactions in your experience. For one thing, progressive conversation was possible if you were capable of it. For another, you learned to look on life as a serious business, to be grappled with, not juggled with — interesting, not merely exciting. Chiefly, the unity of your family and community life awoke and fostered in you solid moral qualities which the nervous metropolitan mind cannot glibly dispose of by calling them stolid. If you had a good many prejudices, you also had some principles. A certain formality and restraint — in its worst phases, a smug respectability — were natural expressions of the common state of mind, just as 'the abandonment of all reticence and dignity' are natural expressions of the other extreme. If you misbehaved with your neighbor's wife, of course you covered it up, not merely because you were a hypocrite, but primarily because your misbehavior ran counter to the life of the family and so was unpardonable in fact as well as in theory.

It is a common mistake to suppose that such life was dull and prosaic. It was just as dull, of course, or as interesting as the family and community were capable of making it. By the same token, the dead uniformity so often ascribed to it was impossible. Families and towns differed from one another; they had to, from their very isolation. It is the modern devices of communication which are making them all alike. The great point to realize, in other words, is that the integrity of the family was the central feature, the informing power of Victorian life. Looking back at it and then beholding disintegrate modern ventures, one is inclined to wonder whether such family integrity isn't, after all, what makes the world go round.

Modern notions of Victorianism, I fear, are too often based on the last vestiges. Survivors are frequently decrepit spinsters — relics rather than exemplars, for the spinster had a poor show in the Victorian scheme of things. But you still find here and there families which retain the central Victorian virtue.

One such family I know. Life to them is a normal and rather serious business, with more humor than wit; never dizzy but also never dull. If they take themselves for granted, it is not because they consider their way of living superior to all others, but because it has never occurred to them that there are other ways — at least for decent, self-respecting people. One even comes to accept their dingy, atrocious drawing-room. It is a sort of natural inheritance for them, like their language with strangers, rather formal and not often used. Yet how they do enjoy life — work and play and the serious business of eating! And their children aren't little prigs at all. They do seem astonishingly dutiful and obedient, but they quarrel with refreshing zest; the boys secretly admire and openly despise the girls; and the girls look on the boys as gluttons — and envy them, as who should say, 'Boys will be boys, and girls would if they could.'

What strikes me most about the grown-ups in this family is the leisurely yet persistent way they go about things — eating, reading (solid, like the food), walking, talking, refraining from talking. If there is an important matter to discuss, they talk it through, with no telephone to stampede them. But they never 'make' conversation; if their talk is persistent, their silence is almost dogged — and no telephone disturbs it, either. I recall wondering once how they kept so full of life when they were so out of touch with the world. 'I mean of course the world of ideas,' I added.

'That depends,' replied my host simply, 'on what you mean by ideas.'

'USE YOUR WRISTES'

CLERGYMEN, even Fundamentalists, are turning more and more to sport for their texts and proverbs. I have heard of one (though I am inclined to disbelieve the libelous yarn) who, meeting with small success in exhorting his congregation not to run after strange gods, made an enormous killing when he shouted, 'It only takes one to hit it.' A pedestrian, therefore, an evolutionist who believes in the Bible, a man who is at once conservative and liberal, and a near relative of the White Knight — such a man scarcely needs to explain that his title, like the clergyman's, isn't the song itself; it's 'only what it's called, you know.'

I have been thinking recently of the sage advice of an old cricket coach. His theme, like that of Chaucer's Pardoner, was 'alwey oon' — 'USE YOUR WRISTES.' It is the advice of the expert, the direct opposite of the popular cry, 'Lay into it.' Yet any one who has followed sport for a number of years has noticed how the emphasis has shifted in favor of the big hitter. What matters a strike-out or two in a crucial moment if the batsman occasionally 'crashes through' with a 'circuit clout'? In golf we are forever thinking of 'laying into it';

156

we have a curiously persistent way of forgetting
that one putt is just as many as one drive. I recall
a bibulous spectator at a big cricket match in
London who shouted, 'Hi loikes to see 'em 'it 'em
blewmin 'igh an' blewmin 'ard an' blewmin often!'
Well, so do we all, I suppose, but it is salutary to
remember also the wisdom of my pockmarked old
friend from Notts: 'Cum on, now. Down't try
to cart it. *Use your wristes.*'

At any rate, his phrase rebukes me every time
I try to 'carry' a bunker that was set up for the
sole purpose of tempting and punishing middle-
aged folk like me. Most of us are trying to be big
hitters all along the line.

The upstanding, two-fisted booster, soberly de-
fining Americanism in terms of size and noise, is
of course our most conspicuous example. But
he's not the only one. The public (to be precise,
99 44/100 per cent of the public) seem to want
shine and speed, at least in automobiles, our chief
national product. Recently I have ridden in the
automobiles of several friends (just to see what it
felt like, of course), and in every one the most
distinctive feature was that you couldn't see
without a periscope. Low, rakish-looking 'speed
boats' they were, no question, but of little value, I
should say, except as museum pieces. My friends
tell me waggishly that they don't have to see, that
it is the pedestrian who must look out. Evidently

157

it isn't a question of where they are going; the prime necessity is to be on the way. To the Gadarene mind, I conclude, 'stepping on the gas' is just the same as 'laying into it.'

Of course I am prejudiced, even bitter, on the subject of motor-cars. But I do recognize that 'laying into it' is very important at times. In public affairs Lincoln certainly laid into it with a vengeance (recall his early comment about hitting slavery — and 'hard too'); but he appears also to have used his 'wristes,' like the good axeman that he was. It is a fair analogy, this figure of the axe. A friend of mine who takes his exercise chopping wood is a delight to behold. So slender is he that you would say he never could split a big stick of oak, but he hits with such neat accuracy, and the head of the axe moves with such a surprising flick just as it enters the wood, that he is a perfect example of what your 'wristes' can do. Roosevelt used to tell a story of how, once when he visited a lumber camp, he spent a day out working with the men. That evening, one of the lumbermen from another group said to Roosevelt's companion. 'Well, Bill, how many d'yuh get?' (meaning trees). 'Forty-nine,' replied Bill. Then, with a jerk of his thumb, 'The colonel here, he *gnawed down* seventeen.'

Sometimes I indulge the hope that our legislators would 'use their wristes' a little. Making law, a disinterested observer might imagine, would imply the skillful building-up of a better *body of law*, repealing foolish laws, amending others, and adding new ones only with great hesitation — a matter for scientific study. Apparently I am wrong. Legislators prefer to lay into it. They must go before their constituents with a quantity record.

These law-makers must be in league with the menu-makers. Doubtless there are restaurants and hotels where you can get a good meal without reading the obituary notice, in Pidgin-French, of all the edible flora and fauna known to man. But such *arcana* are artfully concealed, if not actually padlocked. In most places you encounter quantity, unrelieved by anything resembling a culinary caress. And this large gesture we label, with shameless pride, 'the American Plan.'

The same hard hitting, laborious slugging without finesse, characterizes much of our contemporary literature. I would not be cynical, reader. I have just read an essay on 'Poetry and the Secret Impulse,' by Chauncey Brewster Tinker, who uses both back and wrists to excellent purpose. And one must rejoice that Agnes Repplier, A. Edward Newton, and Samuel Crothers use their wrists brilliantly, even if they don't often hit through the infield. But what is Professor Tinker laying into? A muck-raking biography of Poe, a perfect type of

a book written without wrists. The same characteristic is true of much of our fiction: quantities of
material piled up, pages on pages of evidence to
support puppets who never emerge into characters;
stories which fall to pieces *as stories* just because
they are at bottom only studies in sociology or
pathology. It is refreshing in contrast to turn to
Booth Tarkington, Edna Ferber, and Christopher
Morley, who, if they don't hit very hard, certainly
use their 'wristes.' And John Buchan — but then
he is a Scot, the literary heir of Stevenson, a gentleman with a famous pair of wrists.[1]

Heaven forbid that a mere unmounted layman
should admonish the churches. But isn't there
some knight on wheels or a clergyman on vacation
who might humbly submit that the American
Plan in the churches fails to provide for the still
small voice, that it makes — well, possibly in-
sufficient allowance for what Stevenson called 'the
derisive silence of eternity'?

But there is one activity in America, you might
suppose, which would not yield to the temptation
to lay into it. It is arguable at least, if not altogether obvious, that academic halls have no place
in any scheme of things if they do not put quality
first, last, and all the time. It isn't a question of
having to cheapen your product in order to sell it;

[1] Mayor of Chicago, please admit that Morley's father is an
Englishman!

any university which flirts with quantity production ceases, when the flirtation begins, to be educational. It becomes a manufacturing plant and an employment bureau. Of course the pressure of Alumni for numbers and victories and the pressure of the public for an *abracadabra* which it calls education seems irresistible. But I wonder how irresistible it would appear if our educators emulated Mark Hopkins on the other end of the log. Most of the young men and women who throng our college halls would then feel an irresistible impulse to seek pastures new.

Here, to a Pedestrian mind, is the real cause for cynicism. No use to rail at manufacturers and law-makers and menu-makers when our educational institutions are turning out confirmed addicts to the American Plan. If by some odd turn of the wheel of fortune, my old pockmarked friend from Notts should find himself president of an American University, his inaugural address, I feel certain, would consist of eight words: 'Down't try to cart it. Use your wristes.'

Not such bad advice, either. But he should then hire a dean who could use his toe!

IN A MANNER OF SPEAKING

I HAVE recently been having a bad time of it from those who mistake my vaporings for a philosophy of life. 'What do you mean by "mobocracy"?' writes one correspondent. 'How can you have the effrontery,' writes another, 'to call a drug fiend like Coleridge a pillar of Protestantism?' It had never occurred to me that he was a pillar of Protestantism *because* he was a drug fiend; careless of me not to see that!

I'm afraid, however, that I can't undertake to answer all these and other questions, just as if I were an editor steeped in controversy. In fact, I am inventing a new game, entitled 'Don't Ask Me Another.' I haven't got much beyond the name yet, but it looks as if the rules should be fairly simple. You just say, 'Buzz, buzz, buzz,' and change partners.

There is one communication, though, which I can't withhold. The only trouble with printing it at this point is that it is so good that any poor words of mine which follow must prove an anticlimax. But texts must come first, so here it is.

ET TU?

An 'Advisory Committee,'
Robert Bridges, Shaw the witty,

IN A MANNER OF SPEAKING

Recently has been appointed,
Duly sanctioned and anointed,
To dispense pronunciation
To the docile British nation.

Heralded as lawful masters
Of the radio-broadcasters,
Shall these sacerdotal censors —
These pronuncio-dispensers —
Have their way with me and you?
Stop them, Footpath-man! Ah, do!

Made to go *à deux* with scenery,
Will you tolerate cent*ee*nary?
Is your resolution final
To endure the word doctr*i*nal?
If you swallow eevolution,
Must we take to reevolution?

Though there's nothing new in p*a*tent
Since they've rhymed it long with latent,
When of pat-riots they prate
Are they aching for debate?
If we hide behind our smiles,
Will they pelt us with miss*i*les?

Your eventual decision
On this Oxford-Pshaw revision
Of their late pronunciation,
I await with consternation, —
Fearing, from your Highway, you
May have leanings that way too!

EPILOGUE

So, Pedestrian, won't you say
'Centenary's here to stay?'
Since that's patent, please do add,
'Doctrinal is not so bad!

Missal does for prayers *or* night,
Evolution's plainly right.
As for patriots, that's what we
've always been and mean to be.'
Start a wordy warfare, do,
Take your pen and run them through!
ELIZABETH STANLEY TROTTER

Mrs. Trotter is evidently one of those liberty-loving people who were brought up before the War and who have not adjusted their minds to the new Age of Regulation in which we live and move and lose our being. Post-War conditions allowed a temporary license, to the great debauchery of language and morals, but we have changed all that. If we can't have a political dictator, we're going to have every other kind of dictator. Indeed, the spirit of the age demands more drastic regulation than that proposed by this 'Advisory Committee.' If pronunciation, why not gesture, too? With television the assured fact of to-morrow, radio-broadcasters must be taught, nay, compelled, to suit the action to the word.

Nor would such compulsion be a wholly new thing. Of course, Mrs. Trotter cannot recall the past century, cannot have been brought up, as I was, on a book called 'Lessons in Expression and Physical Drill,' by Darien A. Straw, Chicago, 1892. Evidently she is of more tender years. Perhaps she followed the Montessori Method; probably she does not realize that the liberty-loving period

from which she springs was really of short dura-
tion, that the Mussolini-minded folk of to-day are
harking back to the rigors of the regulated nineties.
The book to which I refer, after serving to confuse
and frighten a small boy thirty-five years ago, now
comes into its own as a priceless historical docu-
ment. It shows what fumbling amateurs Shaw
and his 'Advisory Committee' are, after all.

For Darien A. Straw knew how to regulate not
only speaking, but the manner of speaking, and he
could devise exercises which regulated and per-
fected every gesture, every breath! In his preface,
he quietly asserts that his plan has the advantage
of 'preserving the enthusiasm of the class' and
of 'avoiding weariness of weak bodies or voices.'
Glance, reader, at an exercise or two, and realize
what hardy children we must have been. Here is
part of Lesson XXIV:

178. Speaker's Position. Practice the syllable, *ah*,
expressing the following emotions.
Passionate:

a. Command	f. Chagrin
b. Question	g. Pity
c. Challenge	h. Joy
d. Anger	i. Surprise
e. Apology	j. Fear

When a small boy of thirteen had thoroughly
mastered this step, he was ready with his pre-
served enthusiasm for Lesson XXV, entitled

165

'Laughing Exercise. The Supine Hand.' 'Supine Hand' looks formidable to the adult reader of to-day, but it is defined lucidly for the small boy of yesterday as 'friendy, considerate, and unimpassioned.' Also, in Lesson XXIV he had learned the following simple chart:

Gestures

In Longitude			*In Latitude*
Fr. — Front			Up.
Ob. — Oblique	{	Right — Rt. Left — L.	Upper — U.
Lat. — Lateral	{	Right. Left.	Horizontal — Hor.
Ob. B. — Oblique Backward	{	Right. Left.	Lower — Low.
B. — Backward			Down — D.

Then of course he had already succumbed to Lesson XXII, 'Foot Movement. Sound and Sense,' with this simple diagram:

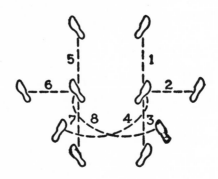

As obfuscation set in, the pupil gradually became proficient in the various kinds of 'Hands' — to wit: Supine, Averse, Index, Prone, Clenched, and Reflex — and knew their symbols backwards. It was therefore a comparatively simple matter for him to render a passage like the following:

> On Linden when the sun was low,
> *Rt. Hor. Fr. Sup.*
> All bloodless lay the untrodden snow;
> *Both Hor. Pr. Fr. to Ob.*
> And dark as winter was the flow
> *Rt. Low. Pr. Av.*
> Of Iser, rolling rapidly.
> *Tracing the course of the river.*

Personally, I must confess that I never quite grasped at thirteen the distinction between the 'Objective' and 'Subjective' eye, nor do I feel now in retrospect that Fig. 27 was a fair illustration of the statement that 'the eye is ordinarily free and flexible in its position, though not vacillating.' Then, too, it must have been rather difficult for fledglings with cracking treble to do justice to the several kinds of tone—Pure, Orotund, Aspirate, Oral, Pectoral, Guttural, Nasal. I submit, moreover (not from any hostility to Mr. Straw, but purely in the interests of a better and brighter education), that Chapter xi was a little early for a study of the 'six definite varieties of Stress.' The word was defined for the edification of ignorant youth as 'the manner in which Force is applied to a tone.' The six definite varieties were illustrated as follows:

a. Radical
b. Median
c. Final
d. Compound
e. Thorough
f. Tremor

These pictures have the conspicuous virtue of being just as easy for a child as for an adult to understand.

Well, Mrs. Trotter, how does your 'Advisory Committee' look now?

Mere *Kinderbrei* to any one who cut his teeth on Darien A. Straw!

Of course, we got some fun out of it. I shall never forget Fred F——, the wag, reciting with due solemnity, appropriate gestures, positions of the feet, tone and stress, and all the 'furniture' —

> My heart lies in the coffin there with Caesar, —
> What cause withholds you then to pass the cheese?

Then there was Commencement and the never-to-be-forgotten image of H. B——, a hearty boy with fat, red hands, who tottered nigh and 'tremored' with palsied voice and 'Up. Rt. F. Pr.' gesture —

IN A MANNER OF SPEAKING

While I've this withered hand to lift,
I'll touch my cap to the proudest man
That faat in the dandy fift.

Time makes those ancient days uncouth, but
Commencement then, bless you, was a genuine
test — of endurance for the audience. Papa in
boiled shirt and frock coat with patent leather
lapels was worn down till he was convinced of the
need of vacation for all concerned. For myself,
I'm inclined to disagree with you, Mrs. Trotter, to
wish for *more* regulation — if only to provoke you
to another poem. In fact, I'm constrained to believe that Bernard Shaw has not lived in vain.

STAR DUST

IF William Lyon Phelps ever writes that book on golf, 'Thirty Years of Looking Up,' as he threatens to do, I claim an inalienable right to pose for the frontispiece. He would probably wish to label the picture with a line from his beloved Browning —

> 'Look thou not down but up!' [1]

> 'To uses of a cup,
> The festal board,' etc.

More definite is the advice of Lady Macbeth —

> 'Only look up *clear*.'

In either case any progress of the golf ball is a fortuitous by-product of the gesture. The golfer who looks steadfastly down peers in vain for a saxpence under the ball ('man, suppose it *had* been there an' ye hadna seen it!') but the golfer whose neck has a permanent wave, who has learned to look up clear, finds not a mere hypothetical saxpence, but the heavens 'inlaid with patines of bright gold.' You don't play golf at night? You might as well, if you look up clear!

Seeing 'the hosts of heaven rise' assumes, of

[1] Browning undoubtedly had golf in mind, perhaps the nineteenth hole. See the next lines —

170

course, that the watcher is outside Scotland or the city of New York. No one can possibly look up clear through Edinburgh murk or the glare of Broadway. In fact, it has long seemed to me that country mice, in their perennial altercation with city mice, neglect their one telling argument. They prate of fresh milk and eggs, but every one knows that fresh things are shipped to the city and that what is left over is returned, in its old age, to the country market. They chatter ecstatically of 'wild life,' yet they know in their hearts that they mean flies and mosquitoes. When the New Yorker asserts calmly that you can find everything under the sun 'right in lil' ole New York,' his country cousin has to admit it; for a man must have an exotic taste who cannot find in New York pretty nearly every product, raw or refined, of the earth on which he lives; and indeed everything *under* the earth too, for in New York he may well say, as did Raleigh after the sack of Cadiz, 'Whoever had a desire to see Hell itself most lively figured, it was there.' But suppose the country cousin should retort: 'Yes, you have everything *under* the sun, but I have everything *over* the sun. Your Harlem goatherds and your Wall Street kings, though it is perhaps a bit grotesque to suppose that they would take any interest in the Star in the East, could not see it if it should haply appear, cannot see it now, this

December, as it rises undenoted over blazing Brooklyn. Pooh! Your "fringes of lamplight, struggling up through smoke and thousand-fold exhalation, ... what thinks Boötes of them, as he leads his Hunting-Dogs over the zenith in their leash of sidereal fire?" You have everything under the sun; I have everything over the sun. I rest my case!'

It is rather astonishing, in view of the fact that there are still some country mice, to find our magazines giving relatively small attention to the wonders of astronomy. Scarcely a month goes by without popular science of every other variety: Do fishes laugh? Do bees see colors? Is your wife descended from a monkey or a spare rib? It is not that astronomy, with its higher mathematics, lacks a popular side. Biology, too, has mysteries unintelligible to the layman, but it gets translated, even the most formidable parts of it, into tabloid form. Surely the magazine reader can swallow 'Aldebaran' and 'parallax' as easily as he gulps 'chromosomes' and 'brachycephalic.' Nor is the relative absence of popular articles on astronomy to be ascribed to its lack of news interest. Not long ago a star very similar in age and composition to our sun exploded in the southern sky. It was forthwith reported that there was no reason whatever why our sun should not indulge in the same sort of antics. This was alarming to any but the philosophic mind, so editors all over the world asked astronomers what would happen to man when, as, and if the sun should explode. 'Well,' says one authority, 'we should know of the explosion in eight minutes and we should have one hundred and thirty-eight hours to live. By that time the burning gases would reach the earth and we should be annihilated.'

Little facts like this develop in us an arresting sense of frailty. But if the newspapers would only go on, we might feel smaller yet. A pedestrian mind must pursue the inquiry, must say, 'Yes, that would be an end of man, but what would become of the sun?' 'Oh,' replies the scientist, 'the sun would resume its normal life; just a few moments of distemper, and then the same old sun again.'

So far the astronomer is using small artillery — just solar system facts. But if this doesn't make us 'blanch with fear,' he can open bigger guns; he can tell us, for instance, and can prove it, that Betelgeuse is so big that, if our sun were at its center, there would be ample room for the earth to move *within the circumference* of the giant star.

One is reminded of the story of a visitor at the Lick Observatory. 'Did you say that those stars are really larger than our sun is, on the average?' 'Yes, sir.' 'Can you give me an idea of how large our sun is?' 'Well, if it were a hollow shell, of its present size, you could pour more than a million earths into it.' 'You say there are possibly or probably planets revolving around many of the cluster stars?' 'Yes, sir.' 'And many of those planets may be inhabited?' 'Yes, sir.' 'Well, then, I think it does not matter very much whether Roosevelt or Taft is nominated next week at the Chicago Convention.'

But feeling small is just the first step in stargazing. In fact, a pedestrian head can't long follow those sentimental poets who remind us every now and then that,

> 'When your fire's last song is sung,
> These old stars will still be young.'

Doctoring Blake, why not cry —

> Taurus, Taurus, who dare frame
> All thy fearful symmetry?
> *Ah, who dare to fashion man,*
> *Curious who hath fashioned thee!*

It seems to me that looking up clear ought not to produce so much a groveling humility as a reverence for the dignity of creation, including man, and I observe that it does have just that effect on astronomers.

It is not for its news value, then, that there should be more popular astronomy and more astronomy in the schools. It is chiefly because it is the most fundamental of the sciences. Recently, since the development of stellar photography and

174

the spectroscope, astronomy has been able to give us plenty of 'news,' but more important than that for the layman is an elementary knowledge of the universe, without which his second-hand reading in derived sciences, such as physics, leads to mechanistic futilities.

Astronomy, furthermore, is so woven into our history, religion, and literature that, far more than any other science, it is part of our mental furniture. The poets have always been busy with it, from Deborah to Alfred Noyes. It is interesting, and mildly instructive too, that, whereas the earlier poets heard the stars shouting and singing, or saw them fighting against Sisera, a modern poet, under the spell of science, writes

'The *silent* firmament marches.'

A little over fifty years ago Tennyson staggered the imagination by the lines —

'Suns along their fiery way,
All their planets whirling round them, flash a million miles a
  day.'

Modern astronomers humbly submit that Arcturus is doing nearly eight million. The same poet wrote

'Twenty millions of summers are stored in the sunlight still';

but careful scientists have recently corrected the figure to ten million million! The poets are often

more picturesque than accurate, but John Hall
Wheelock, who wrote that 'Antares in lone splen-
dour shines,' may not be rebuked by being reminded that Saturn was close to Antares during
most of 1927, for he might retort: 'It looked close
to you, but it was really about three hundred and
fifty light-years away!'

Myths of all peoples are of course bound up with
astronomy, and most religions are full of it. The
star-faiths and the star-superstitions, in fact, have
been the most tenacious. We look with mild contempt on those benighted ancestors of ours who
cast horoscopes and saw disasters in eclipses, but
the majority of people still believe in equinoctial
storms, many are still afraid to sleep under the
moon, and only the other day I heard a gardener
remark: 'They do say that onion sets planted in
the dark of the moon will rise out of the ground on
you.'

Little is more fascinating than the study of the
star-myths in the light of modern science. For if
astronomy dispels the superstitions, it also helps to
account for many of them. One of the most fascinating of these myths, that of the Virgin-birth and
the Star in the East, calls us out to look at the sky
at the Christmas season. John Ruskin ejaculated
the pious wish that he might 'destroy and rebuild
... the East End of London; and destroy, without
rebuilding, ... the city of New York.' Suppose

176

his wish were consummated — after all, a mere
trifle compared to an explosion of the sun. Standing upon the ruins of Broadway, we should see the
heavens at their best season, when, just before
Vega sets, Regulus flashes up over Hellgate, and
ten first-magnitude stars are visible all at once.
The brightest constellation of all is of course
Orion, blazing in the southeastern sky, with Sirius,
brightest star in the heavens, not far to the east-
ward. Now, if we wait till midnight, our myth-
scientists tell us, when Sirius is on the meridian,
we shall see the constellation Virgo just rising over
blackened Brooklyn. It is true that Sirius at that
hour will not be precisely on the meridian, but
somewhat to the left, on account of the Precession
of the Equinoxes; but it was exactly there about
three thousand years ago, when the astronomer-
priests developed the story of the star's connection
with the birth of the sun-god. Christmas midnight, then, was the sacred moment, when the
sun, at the bottom of its lowest swing, was reborn;
and the star directly opposite and symbolic of the
rebirth 'there is little doubt,' says Edward Carpenter, 'is the Star in the East mentioned in the
Gospels.' There is no space here to cite the amazing number of instances, given by Carpenter,
Frazer, and others, in confirmation of this as well
as of its connection with the legend of the Virgin-
birth, not only among the Christians, but among

the Egyptians, Persians, and Arabians; but it is interesting, while we are looking at Orion, to note that French and Swiss peasants are said still to call the three bright stars in his belt, which point straight at Sirius, 'Les trois rois.' By this precession of the equinoxes, moreover, we may account for the fact that the early sacrifices of bull's blood, when the sun was in Taurus at the vernal equinox, gave place about two thousand years later, when the sun had shifted to Aries, to the sacrifice of a he-lamb. One trembles to think what the faithful will do in 4000 A.D., when the zodiacal position of the sun will call for the sacrifice of Aquarius, the water-bearer!

But these applications of astronomy are chiefly amusing, not so earnestly instructive and inspiring as the steady march of those patient and industrious men and women who, with incredible accuracy, measure, weigh, and chart 'the infinite shining heavens' — even globular clusters over two hundred thousand light-years away.

> 'The records grow
> Unceasingly, and each new grain of thought
> Is packed, like radium, with whole worlds of light.
> The eclipses timed in Babylon help us now
> To clock that gradual quickening of the moon,
> Ten seconds in a century.'

A PEDESTRIAN mind is rather averse to creeds and platforms. By its nature it refuses shibboleth, dogma, vicarious thinking. It cannot just step on the gas and skid merrily along the beaten track. It gets no motion from devices; it moves, if slowly, on its own legs.

In one matter, though, the pedestrian has been almost doctrinaire. Stirred by the disposition of most people to generalize life into alternatives, he was early and profoundly convinced that there is a good deal to be said for inclusion, rather than exclusion. More than half the time the sensible course is not to take one side of an issue, but to take both sides. In the first paper of this series he put forward the suggestion that a large part of the acrimony and altercation in our lives springs from our mistaken tendency to take an *either — or* rather than a *both — and* position. We are too prone to contention; we prefer 'argufying' to argument. The whole show over science and religion, for example, gets its support from the contentious bitter-enders. War in the heart, like war on the battle-field, is bred from a malevolent determination to see only one side.

Now this *both — and* state of mind, what

Augustine Birrell called 'catholicity of gaze,' coincides happily with the purposes of 'The Forum' — 'a magazine of controversy.' 'The Forum' believes that there is something to be said for both sides, that in the majority of problems confronting mankind there is no solvent like honest debate. The Editor of 'The Forum' is a dyed-in-the-wool Both — Ander. He knows that Labor and Capital, Science and Religion, Nation and Nation can never settle their differences by biting their thumbs at one another, by taking a most unscientific and a most unreligious *either — or* stand. A friend tells me that she and her husband have an agreement, when they get to using 'never' and 'always' in their altercations, to stop at once; for even if one is right and the other wrong, one cannot use such exclusive language and stay right.

But Pedestrianism is by nature averse to dogma. It is quite possible to be too inclusive. Conceivably there are instances where an intolerant *either — or* position is more honest than an easy-going *both — and* attitude. John Jay Chapman says that we are suffering from a fear complex. And among our various fears, many of us are afraid to stand alone, to walk on our own feet; we must join the crowd, climb aboard some abominable mental bus. Resolute choice of an alternative, where the issue is clear, is of course far better than meek submission. But such meek submission,

it scarcely needs to be pointed out, is not a genuine, *both — and* state of mind. It is not really a
state of *mind* at all; it is a state of heart, or perhaps
of belly, little better than an *either — or* state of
spleen.

The really great danger to a confirmed Both —
Ander, however, is not that he may in his catholicity lose the gift of choice, but that he may lose
the clear vision to cry on occasion, 'A plague o'
both your houses!' Robert Burns and his friends,
in their rustic debating club, were given to argu-
ing such absurd propositions as the question
whether it was better to marry a pretty girl with
a bad character or an ugly girl with a good character. In spite of the fact that Burns in his private
practice appears to have viewed this question
with a disastrous catholicity, the young men in
the club argued with a seriousness which implied
hope of solution; they were clearly committed to
an *either — or* state of mind. It does not seem to
have occurred to them that both time and energy
might have been saved by an emphatic '*Neither
— nor*'! For years I tried to decide whether I preferred an upper or a lower berth in a sleeping-car.
Obviously I couldn't use both; I supposed I must
choose one or the other. But I learned, in course
of time, that they were only specious alternatives,
that the real solution was '*neither — nor.*'

It might be salutary to apply the same answer

181

to a good many important questions confronting us nowadays. *Either — or* usually prolongs the issue; *both — and* is better, but though it softens the issue, it frequently fails to remove it; *neither — nor* has the virtue of clearing the air. 'You are wrong and I am right' is a dangerous speech. 'We're both partly right,' the instinct of the Both — Ander, may save the day. But 'We're both wrong, absolutely and absurdly wrong' brings a new day.

Among the alternatives recently offered to us is the unsatisfactory choice between the saloon and prohibition. Ignoring the suspicion that we are in fact getting both, we have good cause to resent the assumption that the alternative to prohibition is the saloon. Yet fear that it is supports many a pallid prohibitionist. What's the matter with *neither — nor?*

Another hoary notion is that lack of efficiency spells inefficiency. It is about as sensible as to say that pessimism is the only alternative to optimism. The opposite of efficiency may be genius. Consider the story of the old negro cook. Asked by a little girl how much molasses she put in her cookies, she replied, 'Jest enough, honey.' Was she efficient? Not a bit of it. Take a cook book and measure and work till you eliminate mistakes; then you will make very good cookies — but they won't be a patch on the work of a culinary genius. For though you can with perseverance make good cookies, you can't ever be a first-class cook; nor, for that matter, can you be an efficient gardener in any important sense. In fact, there are so many important things, like making love or taking a walk, which have nothing whatever to do with the question of efficiency that it is an impertinence to subject man to a formula.

In public affairs the most conspicuous *either — or* delusion just now is the notion that the nations of Europe, perhaps America too, must choose between Black and Red. Not only monarchy, we are told, but constitutional democracy is doomed. Man must abandon the notion that he can ever learn to govern himself; the day of the dictator, whether Black or Red, is at hand. It emerges very soon, in any discussion of these two colors, that they are not very different, that they both spell dictatorship and regimentation; in other words, that the choice is not between them, but, *da capo*, between Absolutism and Liberalism.

Well, let it go at that, say the jingoes. Liberalism is discredited; the alternative is Absolutism, and so you come back to a choice between Fascism and Communism. It is a plausible argument, but it deals largely in what rhetoricians used to call *petitio principii*. It is quite conceivable, of course, that the facts in Europe just at the present time discredit man's gradual development of constitu-

183

tional Democracy; the failure of so-called Democracy is painfully conspicuous. But that does not discredit *Liberalism* — by a long shot. Just because nineteenth-century Democracy, an alleged form of Liberalism, has failed, there is no reason to suppose that all other forms of Liberalism must fail. Nor is it any more reasonable to suppose that Communism and Fascism are the only available forms of Absolutism.

It may well be that further experiments in Communism and Fascism will have to be made before people discover that the cure is worse than the disease. People have wanted to be bossed before — have clamored for a Cæsar in the past. They may get an able Cæsar; but the fallacy, now as then, lies in the fact that such rule is inevitably temporary. It cannot perpetuate its virtues; there is no possible chance for progress. The method sooner or later means a Louis XV — and then the deluge.

The real issue, if there must be alternatives, is between Liberalism and Absolutism, and in that case there is possible an emphatic choice, an *either — or* decision. But there is no real choice, because there is no vital distinction, between Fascism and Communism. It is mere journalistic jugglery to pretend that the world, or even Europe, is to be engulfed in a decision between two fictions — one already discredited, a shabby pinkish red,

184

the other, a shiny but not durable black, coterminous with the life of the Italian man of destiny. It is preposterous to assume that the human mind can devise no way out, to suppose that man is forever committed to Tweedledum or to Tweedledee.

Once upon a time there was a restaurant with the placarded promise that it purveyed coffee and pie 'just like mother used to make.' A hungry passer-by entered and asked about the coffee and the pie.

'Are they really "just like mother used to make"?' he said.

'Yes, sir,' replied the proud proprietor — '"just like mother used to make."'

'Very well,' said the customer. 'I think I'll have a sandwich and a cup of tea.'

RELIGIO PEDESTRIS

So the heart be right, it is no matter which way the head lies. — RALEIGH to his executioner.

THE Reverend Studdert Kennedy (Saint 'Woodbine Willie') says in a stimulating article in the November 'Forum' that 'the great necessity for democracy is a true religion.' He adds that this idea 'will bear a lot of thinking about.' He is right. A number of people have been thinking about it, off and on, for a good many years and haven't worn it down yet.

It's a very provocative thought — no question. The difficulty, now as ever, is to get at the word *religion*. Religion, Mr. Kennedy says, is 'a synthesis and sublimation of all the instincts.' There is a fork in the road here; in fact, a veritable five corners. It would be inviting to stroll down the road of the 'sublimated instincts' and find out where it comes from. (People, by the way, have a curious habit of following paths to see whither they lead, whereas oftener than not the vital question is whence they come.) Then there is another road, with Professor Irving Babbitt at the entrance, waving his arms and beckoning to the place where impulse is not sublimated, but is checked by the *frein vital*, where 'natural' law

186

is regulated by 'human' law. 'Very good,' the Saint might retort; 'only' — but I'm not going to let these philosophers involve me in a controversy; especially as I hear an Oriental gentleman at another road, warning me that 'the West still believes that knowledge will give her God.' His road is rather more alluring, with its camels and palanquins and far-off temples shimmering through the dust; and his voice has a mysterious charm as he tells me, without waving his arms, that religion is not a matter of instincts, sublimated or restrained, but of losing our wills in the Will of the Universe. It was a man from that region who said, 'Beware, beware: good can choke up a soul as much as evil.' And *that* 'will bear a lot of thinking about.'

I shan't describe the other roads; for, as I look again more closely, I see that there are more than five — myriads, indeed, and all good roads, I have no doubt. But if you take your religion afoot, you follow the footpath way — sometimes an easier, simpler way; sometimes too, the more hardy pedestrians avouch, an arduous, lonely way. I speak not from much experience, but report truly what other pedestrians, those of the better sort, have told me. Backslider that I am, I am more familiar with religion of the highway.

Religion is a complicated, a forbidding thing when it gets confused with philosophy or theology.

187

It is a hideous thing when it appears in the discordant din of 'sects and schisms.' Usually, it is a tawdry thing. Yet, stripped of its derivative meanings, religion becomes so simple and so fundamental that there is nothing in it for the controversialists to write about. This simple, inevitable 'tie that binds' — back through the experience of mankind to the source of life itself — all men recognize it without definition in those rare moments when they accomplish true humility. But they are bound to lose sight of it if they mistake groveling for humility, or if they seek to pass reforms in the name of religion, or to formulate creeds, or to bite their thumbs at one another.

Of course it may be charged that one who takes his religion afoot is incapable of the exhilaration that impels your regular 'go-getter' Christian. But it has its compensations. A pedestrian in his wanderings stops in a good many wayside churches; sometimes, too, in little chapels among the hills; and of course he has long been aware that

'The groves were God's first temples.'

In these places — the pretentious 'church edifice,' the modest little chapel, and the far-flung forest aisles — he finds a good deal of religion in its purest and simplest sense. It doesn't seem to make much difference to religion what sort of outward stage men set for it. Non-conformists have

time out of mind mocked the audacity of tradi-
tionalists for supposing that 'consecration' made
bricks and mortar holy; but they also have to
learn that the mere lack of consecrated stones
does not in itself invoke the Holy Spirit. The
groves were also the devil's first hunting-grounds.

It is not unnatural, therefore, that religion in
derivative senses, terrible or tawdry, should
flourish too in all three types of places. With or
without buildings, man seems to find adequate opportunity to glorify himself and to hold public
altercations with his Maker. What the pedestrian
notices most, however, is a kind of religiosity, a
sort of seething, potential current, dammed by
vain imaginations, made impotent and unholy
by self-assertion rather than strong and beneficent
by humility. 'Vanity is the worst impurity.'

But we must not fall into the common error of
cynical youth and denounce all the forms and
trappings that frequently stifle 'pure religion.'
Sometimes they do just the reverse — set the
current going. In any event, the social animal,
man, cannot get along without some outward
and visible sign. Even the superstitions are better
than nothing. Most of us, if we face the facts,
must have some sort of idol — even if we make it
of mental mud. Worship of almost anything is
better than no worship at all; in fact, no worship
at all, the metaphysicians tell us, is really worship

of the devil (*der Geist der stets verneint*)! With the *forms* of religion there can be no sensible quarrel. Personally, I am so far a Protestant that I think there are not forms enough. Inclined for the most part to the Quaker 'way,' as less obstructive, I crave at times a more outward expression, a more objective beauty; at other times I wish for a positive hilarity in my religion. Yet I am not permitted to belong to a number of churches, as I might to a number of clubs — to the Society of Friends, for instance, to the Roman Catholic Church, and to the Holy Rollers all at once. It seems to me a very narrow dispensation.

If such genuine catholicity were permitted, we might go even further: we might learn from the East something about holiness. I don't mean that there is anything promising in the gesture of certain exotic Christians, who dabble in Eastern cults. In the first place, they are playing at religion. In the second, they mistake cogitation for meditation. You in the West, says a Holy Man of India, are 'no more capable of meditation than a tiger is of vegetarianism.' Furthermore, I can't see why an Occidental should try to become an imitation Buddhist any more than a Hindu should try to become a 'go-getter' Christian. Indeed, I do not see why the East and the West cannot be complementary in this as in other things. In the East, religion in its essential meaning must imply meditation. Is it wholly fanciful to imagine that in the West it must imply passion? God may appear in the whirlwind as well as in the still small voice. The Reverend Samuel Drury once preached a sermon, of great appeal to me, on the necessity of 'ambulatory and ejaculatory prayer.' The great point in the West is to invade activity with religion, not evade activity for religion.

Still, lacking the guiding and elevating power of meditation, our passion too often takes the course of sound and fury. It was Nicholas Farrar, I think, a gentle soul of the seventeenth century, who went into seclusion at Little Gidding to escape what he called the 'furie of Protestantism.' Perhaps the latest manifestation of that fury is the disposition to discuss religion, to imagine, on the one hand, that a sort of Rotary Club conference will settle the matter once and for all; or, worse yet, to indulge in obstreperous vilifications — which may well strike the poor benighted heathen as odd interpretations of Christ's teachings. I fear that the trouble usually begins in the pulpit. Instead of feeding the hungry sheep, the clergy indulge freely the quaint notion that they are called upon to deliver lectures on all sorts of social, economic, and political questions. They too often turn the pulpit into a sort of Union Square soapbox. Cynical and flamboyant youth ought to be allowed to heckle then and there, and so get it over with instead of filling the magazines with their controversies. Of course the controversies may be all right, as such, but they are not religion. As Godkin said at the outbreak of the Spanish War, 'Why drag God into it?'

'Woodbine Willie' is right. We need 'true religion.' What seems to stand in the way of it, though, is not some mysterious new malady of democratic peoples, but the old, old malady. The air is still full of discord, in the name of religion.

Yet — we have a strange and promising way of dropping our bickerings at Christmas. Those to whom the day means more than feasting and exchanging gifts recognize in it only one significance — peace on earth, good will toward men. It never enters the head of Romanist or Protestant on that day that the other belongs to a perverse generation of vipers. Each, without reservations or theological distinctions, is celebrating the birth of Jesus; each accepts entirely, without quibble, the message symbolized by that birth—peace on earth, good will toward men.

But what preposterous person would suggest seriously that we try the Christmas religion for three hundred and sixty-five days a year? It would play havoc with our vilifications. It might destroy our precious institutions. What it might do for democracy and mankind surpasses the wildest dreams. It would mean unheard-of effort, impossible renunciation, incredible Grace. Yet — Christmas is not an effort, and on that day Grace is had for the asking!

DUST AND ASHES

IT is with professed regret and secret gladness that we announce our inability to make the 'Footpath and Highway' pages into a genuine 'Column.' Give and take is delightful in a daily and possible in a weekly, but the issue is cold by the time a monthly can print columniations. For this, much thanks! When the issue is hot, you say what you feel, not what you think; and then you spend an amiable aftermath explaining that what you said wasn't what you meant. Ordinarily, therefore, we cannot serve in these pages the funeral baked meats which our friends and enemies send us. But we mean just this once to honor our rule in the breach. We cannot pass lightly over a definite prediction of our demise.

It's a long road that has no turning; and our enemies will rejoice to learn, if the following prediction is correct, that ultimately 'Footpath and Highway' must come to an end. In Hatchards's 'The Books of To-day and the Books of To-morrow,' for October, 1925, the following verses appear:

A —TH CENTURY CONVERSATION

Between a Synthetic Baby and its Father

Goo! what's that ancient print, Daddy —
That funny-looking man?

DUST AND ASHES

The species is extinct, laddy,
   That's a pedestrian.

Whatever is a 'destrian, Daddy?
   (Tut, how the child does talk!)
A twentieth-century nuisance, laddy,
   A boob who used to walk.

I've never heard of 'walk,' Daddy,
   Is it in any book?
The word has disappeared, laddy,
   So there's no need to look.

And what are those queer things, Daddy,
   That from his body grow?
They called them 'arms' and 'legs,' laddy,
   Some centuries ago.

Did people *use* their legs, Daddy,
   When all the world went wrong?
Only a few poor muts, laddy,
   That's how some got along.

And what about the rest, Daddy?
   (Goo! hist'ry gets me thrilled!)
They rode in autocars, laddy,
   Till all who 'walked' were killed. . . .

Goo! what a body! Look, Daddy!
   So big and fat and round!
Men used to eat gross meats, laddy,
   Their stomachs were renowned.

And what a tiny head, Daddy,
   Not HUGE like yours and mine!
Quite large enough for brains, laddy,
   In 1929.

I'm glad *I* didn't live, Daddy,
  In such a savage age!
Those were the bad old days, laddy,
  So says our greatest sage.

And what's the blighter's name, Daddy? —
  Hush — speak of him with awe!
He's called the New Methuselah, laddy,
  Methuselah Bernard Shaw.

These lines stir in us a strange emotion, such as a man might have on reading his own epitaph. We feel like Partridge, the quack astrologer, whom Swift so successfully condemned to death-in-life. When the date came round on which, according to Swift's prediction, Partridge was to die, the poor fellow protested in vain that he was alive and kicking. For ourselves, though, we take comfort in the reflection that it were noble to die if we could thereby win immortality for Bernard Shaw. More than this, we take positive courage when we realize that only the physical pedestrian is doomed. Mental pedestrianism, we venture to predict, may still flourish in those ultimate days. It was that which we championed at the start, in despite of the flivverous mind, and we still dare to hope that it will persist, even among the synthetes. In fact, we are inclined, while we are quoting poetry, to add the lines from an old doggerel, which supplied us with the first article of our pedestrian creed. The verses appear to be anonymous, though they were for a long time erroneously attributed to Snodgrass:

> 'The path of honest thinking, —
> That way afoot you go;
> There isn't any engine
> Will cross the rock and snow.'

The author of these lines of course never dreamed of the aeroplane. But that engine, we observe, skips the elementary steps and often comes to grief in the end. Our creed is unshaken.

Poetry appears to be the order of the day. A great man has recently noticed the fact, asking somewhat sadly why people cannot leave poetry, as they do other things, to specialists and experts. At first blush, perhaps, it is a matter for sad reflection that poetry and politics are still left to amateurs. But such gloom springs from the popular fallacy that efficiency is the opposite of inefficiency — true enough, possibly, in the manufacture of things, but an absurd assumption in affairs of passion, like poetry and politics.

Well, to make a clean breast of it, we have been versifying ourselves. God shield man that we should pretend it is poetry, but we hoped great things for it till our Poetry Editor told us it was 'not available,' or 'not suited to his present needs' — we forget which contemptible phrase he used. Not available indeed! There it was on his desk, offered 'at your usual rates' — with ten per cent off for cash. Not suited to his present needs, i' sooth! The theme is universal. We expostulated, and he thereupon, mistaking us for a humorist, offered to accept the verses if we would omit the first four stanzas! Then, seeing that we were still unsubdued, he quoted with eloquent eye-brows an almost true *dictum* of our own — '"Poetry is fire, which, if harmless, is ashes."' 'This,' he added with deliberation and with that compassionate look peculiar to editors — 'this — is — harmless.'

But we were undefeated. Anger and despair soon yielded to cunning. Why not print the verses in 'Footpath and Highway'? Ha! Revenge! Far sweeter than the 'usual rates'! Quoting the Poetry Editor in one of his less happy moments, we cried — '"Od's blood! I'll do't myself!"'

THE FOOTPATH WAY

The old path, the worn path,
With a pack upon your shoulder —
Oh, there are pleasant places
    For walking men to know;
So sing your catch the bolder
Across the meadow spaces,
Along the highway places,
    That lead where men should go.

The old path, the dim path,
With fairy feet that patter —
Oh, there are magic places
    Adown the ferny glen;

DUST AND ASHES

But turn you with your clatter,
For these are secret spaces,
The children's special places,
   And never meant for men.

The old path, the steep path,
To the dizzy ridges clinging —
Oh, there are toilsome places
   For walking men apart;
You've lost your breath for singing,
But the song of open spaces,
Of jagged skyline places,
   Is working in your heart.

The new path, the hard path,
With a pack upon your shoulder, —
Oh, there are lonely places
   For walking men to go;
Above the scrub and boulder —
Dawn-transfigured spaces,
Stern and starlit places —
   And it's these that you shall know!

THE END